Mel Bay Presents

American & Country Music Tune Book

by
Kenneth
P. W. Rainey

Cover photo credit: © Digital Vision

Visit us on the Web at http://www.melbay.com — E-mail us at email@melbay.com

Contents

Introduction

Although orality has long been a defining trait of many of the diverse traditions in the rural American South, tunebooks have also helped to shape the repertoire. Shape-note hymnals have been a major force in shaping Southern musical culture. The rise of mass-marketed rural culture brought literate influences to secular music as well. When the Depression virtually eliminated the "hillbilly" record market, popular radio barn-dance stars such as Bradley Kincaid augmented their income by selling inexpensive tunebooks to their legions of fans. The scholarship of collectors such as Child and Sharp as well as countless other folklorists has also filtered back into rural America.

The Urban Folk Revival of the 1960s spawned innumerable publications of "traditional" music, focusing primarily upon what were (often incorrectly) assumed to be folksongs. Revivalists and scholars frequently had folkloric prejudices which were not shared by the people they studied. Hence, most tunebooks presented an extremely limited portrait of the music they purported to represent. Instrumental music was largely neglected. Although Tin-Pan Alley tunes had frequently found their way into the oral repertoire, they were seldom represented. And while commercial country music played an increasingly important role in rural American music culture, it is almost wholly excluded from later tunebooks.

Beyond the matter of repertoire, many modern tunebooks present the material in illegible formats, utilizing novel yet indecipherable notation systems, and are filled with transcription errors and tunes presented in unidiomatic keys. As I became increasingly interested in teaching and performing this music, I saw a need for a new tunebook that was suitable for both purposes. This effort is an attempt to improve upon those earlier works.

This book contains 118 tunes. It contains ballads, old-time fiddle tunes, work songs, play songs, hymns and spirituals, rags and blues. It contains tunes from the early commercial period of country music, from traditional material performed by groups like Charlie Poole's North Carolina Ramblers and Gid Tanner's Skillet Lickers to Cliff Carlisle tunes to western swing as recorded by Bob Wills and Milton Brown. Many have never been published in any other tunebook.

Format

The transcriptions contained herein are prescriptive rather than descriptive. They are not intended to represent everything that happened in a recorded performance down to the microtonal variances of every string bend. Instead, they are modeled after the "Real Book" in that they intend to communicate, as clearly and concisely as possible, the information a performer needs to play the tune. When possible, tunes and lyrics appear on a single page. Any multiple-page tunes are laid out in such a manner that no page turns are necessary. I have made every effort to make the formatting of the transcription reflect the structure of the tune for ease of reading. Tunes with four-measure phrases, for example, have been laid out (whenever possible) so that each system has four measures and sections are clearly marked.

I have tried to make the transcriptions as clear and easy to read as possible. In tunes with repeated sections, I've avoided including first and second endings. The difference between first and second endings in this music is minimal—a difference in pick-up notes. Notes in parentheses at the end of a repeated section are the pickup to the next section. In tunes with predominant triplet or swing rhythm, I have made a mention of it with expressions above the first staff rather than write the lopsided triplet rhythm out in full for every occurrence. The text is no smaller than 12-point type. Call-and-response background vocals are marked with parentheses.

A few well-known vocal numbers, such as "Beautiful Dreamer" and "Home on the Range," are included as instrumental waltzes for practical reasons. Few people, myself included, know enough waltzes, and these are two well-known and fairly easy tunes that work well for contra dancing.

Methodology

Most of the tunes presented here were transcribed from commercially available recordings, many of them reissues of old 78 RPM records recorded in the late 1920s and early 1930s. This presents some basic problems to the transcriber. Country musicians seldom tuned to "standard" pitch. Singers tune and capo to suit their range. 78 RPM records were generally designed to play in the neighborhood of 78-80 RPM, but it can sometimes be difficult to discern the exact speed at which a master was made. The end result of this is that it can be tricky initially to determine what key some tunes are in. If a recording of a fiddle tune is in A Flat, a key few old-timers would ever mess with, it takes a bit of experimenting to figure out if the piece was played in G or A. In such cases, the more idiomatic key won out.

In many cases, such as "Banks of the Ohio," a song has been recorded in several different keys to accommodate different vocal ranges. In these situations, the key used for the transcription is a matter of personal preference and current practice. When interpreting these transcriptions, performers should feel free to pitch a song so that it fits comfortably within their vocal range, as this is a perfectly acceptable and common practice in this tradition.

With older recordings, it can sometimes be difficult to hear background instruments, making it a bit of a challenge to pick out chord voicings and harmonic progressions. In cases where this was particularly difficult, additional recordings were consulted. In situations where this wasn't possible, decisions were made based upon what is idiomatic for the instruments involved and what is stylistically consistent with the norms of the genre.

Lastly, it can be difficult to decipher lyrics from older recordings. When a lyric was difficult to understand, additional recordings were consulted. If that proved fruitless, I made an educated guess. Beyond the matter of unraveling texts, there is the additional matter of changing values making certain sentiments expressed in older songs inappropriate for modern performances. Both black and white performers sprinkled their verses with epithets like "nigger," darkie," "coon," and so on. In those cases, I substituted a sentiment consistent with the tone of the song that doesn't carry the same pejorative connotations. For example, in "Ham Beats All Meat," Dr. Humphrey Bates and his Possum Hunters sing the following:

> *White folks in the dining room, eating on mutton and lamb*
> *Darkies in the kitchen, goin' for that good sweet ham*

Such sentiments are justifiably offensive to modern ears. In transcribing the song, I replaced the offending lyric with "While *you're* in the dining room, eating on mutton and lamb, *I'll* be in the kitchen, goin' for that good sweet ham." While still insensitive to vegetarians (to whom I suggest singing "tofu beats textured vegetable protein"), the new lyric is syllabically correct and doesn't promote racial dietary stereotypes. It is not my intention to censor history, but rather to construct a tunebook which can be used for pedagogic and public performance purposes. A typical bar gig is not the best place to dredge up the ugly underbelly of America's past.

The Last Word

One final difficulty in transcribing music from an oral tradition is the possibility that the transcription might be thought of as representing the authoritative version of the tune. Many of these transcriptions are composites, based upon several different recordings, taking a little from each. Others are my own arrangements of tunes common to the repertoire. Many of the tunes presented here exist in several versions, each substantially different from the other. Different tunes may share the same title, and a single tune might be known by any number of different names. Verses float freely from tune to tune. These cheat sheets are meant to be a starting point for the performance of this music. I have included information about reissues of this music at the end of this volume, and I hope that anyone interested in learning to play this music will track down the older recordings to appreciate the remarkable variety that exists within these traditions.

A Guide to Transposition and a Word About the Capo:

Although the capo is referred to derisively as a "cheater" in some circles, it can be a valuable tool—handy for the guitarist, almost essential to the banjo player. Capos are also available for mandolins and other stringed instruments (even DOBROs®), and these might prove handy for beginning players. When buying a capo, avoid the cheap elastic variety, as they can be hard to use and tend to pull the instrument out of tune. I prefer the "one-hand" spring-action capo, such as a Keyser, for ease of use, although there are a number of well-made capos in different styles on the market which will do the trick for under twenty dollars, Dunlop and Shubb being two of the more popular brands.

The reasons for using a capo are quite simple. You may need to transpose a song to accommodate a singer's range. You may find yourself playing with folks who play familiar tunes in unfamiliar keys. Most commonly, however, you may find that you need access to notes on open strings to play a tune comfortably.

In guitar playing, the ideal flatpicking keys are C and G. These are also the two easiest keys on the five-string banjo in standard tuning. The trick to using the capo, then, is using it to play tunes in other keys as though they were in C or G. The process is quite easy once you get the hang of it. Just count up from the nut in half-steps. To play in D, capo on the second fret and play as if you were in C. To play in A, capo on the second fret and play as if you were in G. To play in B Flat, capo on the third fret and play as if you were in G, and so on.

Most old-time songs use a limited number of chords—a "tonic" or I chord, which represents the home key; a "dominant" or V7 chord which tends to show up near the end of phrases and is used to lead back to the tonic; and a "subdominant" or IV chord, a whole step below the dominant, which is used to add some variety to the mix.

Here are the I, IV and V7 chords for the most commonly encountered keys:

	I	IV	V7
A Major:	A(I)	D(IV)	E7(V7)
A minor:	A minor(i)	D minor(iv)	E7(V7)
C Major:	C(I)	F(IV)	G7(V7)
D Major:	D(I)	G(IV)	A7(V7)
D minor:	D minor(i)	G minor(iv)	A7(V7)
E Major:	E(I)	A(IV)	B7(V7)
F Major:	F(I)	B Flat(IV)	C7(V7)
G Major:	G(I)	C(IV)	G7(V7)

Thus, if you want to play a tune in D as though it were in C, capo on the second fret and play C, F, and G7. With the capo in place, they will sound as D, G, and A7. With a little bit of practice, a capo can make your life a lot easier.

Alabama Bound

I'm A - la - ba - ma bound

A - la - ba - ma bound

I got a mule to ride if the train breaks

down

If my mule won't go
Honey don't you talk
`Cause I'm going to Alabama if I have to walk

Lord the preacher got drunk
Threw his bible down
And the congregation said he's Alabama bound
Chorus

I went to the levee
There I learned to skin
Lord I made good money but I threw it all in
Chorus

If your woman leaves you
Boy don't you wear no black
Some cold frosty morning she'll come hobbling back
Chorus

And I've had a good time
That I'll have to agree
But you see what booze has done to me
Chorus
(Repeat first verse)

All Night Long Blues

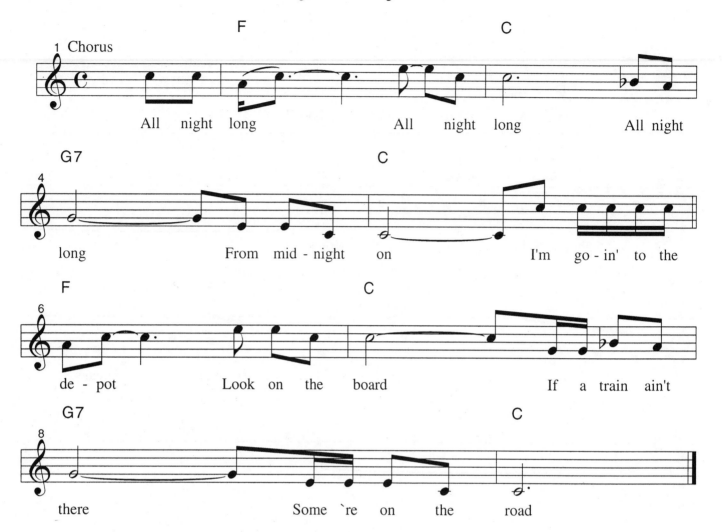

1 Chorus — All night long   All night long   All night
long   From mid-night on   I'm go-in' to the
de-pot   Look on the board   If a train ain't
there   Some 're on the road

Some `re on the road
Some `re on the road
If a train ain't there
Some `re on the road

If I'd a minded
What mama said
I woulda been sleeping
In mama's bed
All night long
All night long
All night long
From midnight on

But me being young
And foolish too
I left my home
On account of you
On account of you
On account of you
I left my home
On account of you

I'd rather be dead
And in my grave
Then be in this town
Treated this a-way
All night long
All night long
All night long
From midnight on

Ain't got no woman
Ain't got no kin
Ain't go nobody
To be bothered with
All night long
All night long
All night long
From midnight on

So if I live
And don't get killed
I'll make my home
In Louisville
All night long
All night long
All night long
From midnight on

All night long
All night long
All night long
From midnight on

Arkansas Traveler

Banks of the Ohio

I asked my love to take a walk
Just a lit - tle ways with me
And as we walked then we would talk
All a - bout our wed - ding day

Chorus:
Oh darling say that you'll be mine
In our home we'll happy be
Down beside where the waters flow
On the banks of the Ohio

I took her by her pretty white hand
And led her down those banks of sand
I pushed her in where she would drown
And watched her as she floated down
Chorus

Returning home between twelve and one
Thinking Lord, what a deed I've done
I've killed the girl I love you see
Because she would not marry me
Chorus

The very next day about half past four
The sherrif knocked on my front door
Come now boy, for you must go
Down to the banks of the Ohio
Chorus

Beautiful Dreamer

Beaumont Rag

Been to the East, Been to the West

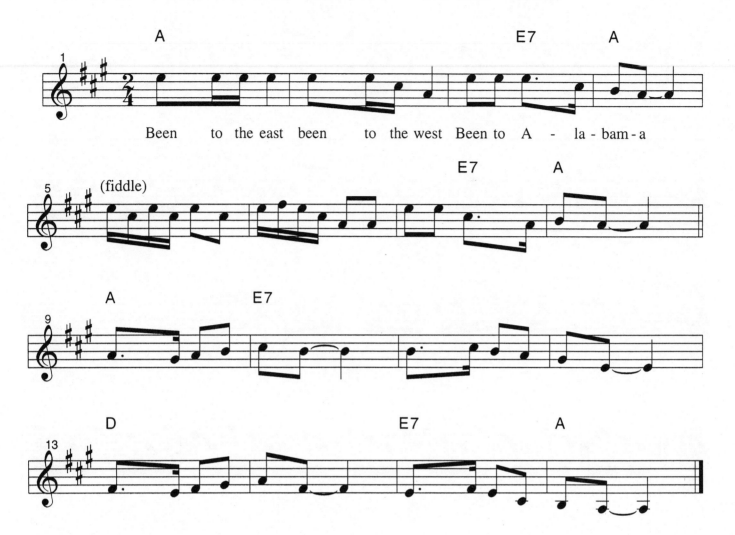

Been to the east been to the west Been to A - la - bam - a

I've got a gal, pretty as can be
She lives in Alabama

You want to know her name, I'll tell you what it be
Her name is Louisiana

(Repeat first verse)

Prettiest gal I ever did see
Lives in Alabama

Bile Them Cabbage Down

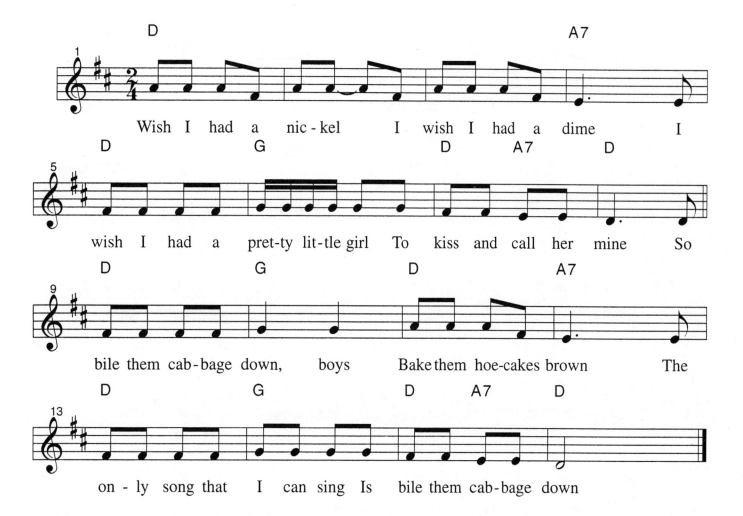

All I need is a pig in the pen
And the corn to feed him on
Pretty little woman to stay at home
And feed him when I'm gone
Chorus

But when I went to see my gal
This is what she said
Said I wouldn't marry you
If the rest of the boys were dead
Chorus

The river is wide and the channel is deep
The wind blows steady and strong
All I want is a little greenback
To push my boat along
Chorus

I went across the river
I crossed it on a swing
I was getting to the other side
You could hear my banjo ring
Chorus

Bill Cheatham

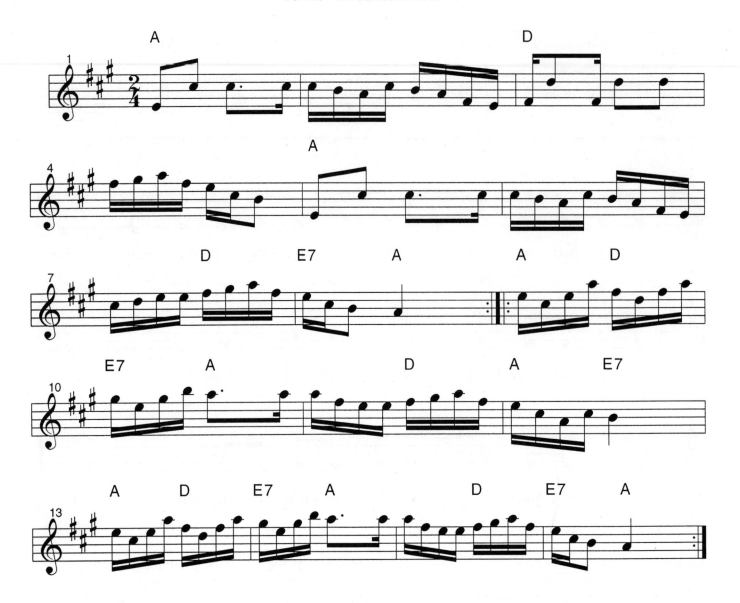

Blue Eyes

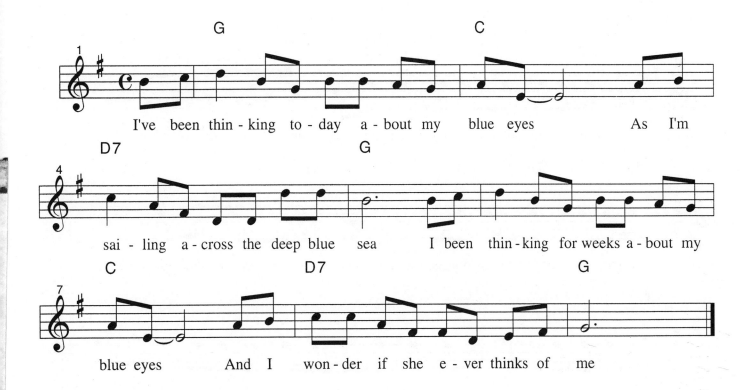

I've been thin-king to-day a-bout my blue eyes As I'm
sai-ling a-cross the deep blue sea I been thin-king for weeks a-bout my
blue eyes And I won-der if she e-ver thinks of me

T'would been better for us both had we never
In this wide and wicked world had never been
For the pleasure we've both seen together
I'm sure love I'll never forget
Chorus

Oh you told me once dear that you loved me
You said that we never would part
But a link in the chain has been broken
Leaves me with a sad and aching heart
Chorus

When the cold, cold grave shall enclose me
Will you come dear and shed just one tear
And say to the strangers around you
Of the heart you have broken, my dear
Chorus

If I had white wings like an angel
All around this wide world I would fly
I would fly into the arms of my dear blue eyes
And right there I'd be willing to die
Chorus

Bring it on Down to My House

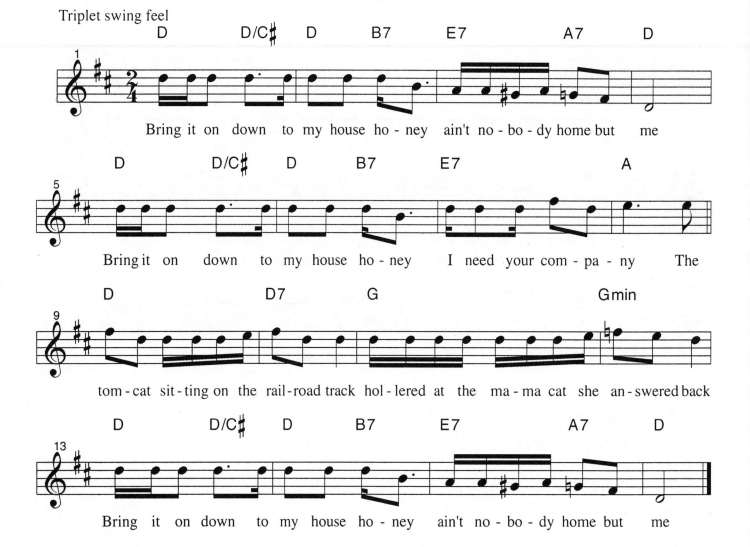

Triplet swing feel

(Verse 1)
Bring it on down to my house ho-ney ain't no-bo-dy home but me

Bring it on down to my house ho-ney I need your com-pa-ny The

tom-cat sit-ting on the rail-road track hol-lered at the ma-ma cat she an-swered back

Bring it on down to my house ho-ney ain't no-bo-dy home but me

Bring it on down to my house honey, ain't nobody home but me
Bring it on down to my house honey, I need your company
My gal Sal, she makes good pie
Ate so much I nearly died
Bring it on down to my house honey, ain't nobody home but me

Bring it on down to my house house honey, ain't nobody home but me
Bring it on down to my house honey, I need your company
Jack and Jill went up the hill
I don't know what they're up to but they're over there still
Bring it on down to my house honey, ain't nobody home but me

Bring it on down to my house honey, ain't nobody home but me
Bring it on down to my house honey, I need your company
Say old man, can you play the fiddle
If you buy me whiskey then I can play a little
Bring it on down to my house honey, ain't nobody home but me

Carroll County Blues

Chicken Roost Blues

Late last night I went to town To get me a chic-ken or two

When I heard the old shot-gun I sure did ski-doo

Grabbed my sack and I made for the door But I did-n't get a-way in time

As I went a-round the cor-ner of the barn Boy I sure got mine Yo-de-

le-hee-ho the chic-ken roost blues

The guy who shot at me last night
Must've been a hard-boiled old squirt
`Cause when the buckshot hit the seat of my pants
Boy they sure did hurt

When I got home, I went to bed
But I couldn't sleep at all
For every time I would close my eyes
I could hear that rooster squall
Odelay-hee-ho, the rooster's squall

I got up, I was sittin' by the fire
When I heard someone outside
They come in the gate and up on the porch
I almost jumped out of my hide

The Sherrif come up and he knocked on the door
Long about half-past two
I said Mr. Sherrif, what do you want
He says I've come for you
Odelay-hee-ho, I've come for you

Grabbed my pants, I jumped out the window
And I started off to run
About that time, he grabbed me by the collar
Said I've got you, son-of-a-gun

Here in the jail for ninety days
And it's home home sweet home to me
I'll get me another sack of chickens
The day that I get free
Odelay-hee-ho, the day that I get free

Cindy

I went up to the mountain
To give my horn a blow
I thought I heard my Cindy say
Yonder comes my beau
Chorus

Cindy went a-preaching
She shouted and she squealed
She got so full of glory
She tore her stocking heel
Chorus

I wish I was an apple
Hanging from a tree
And every time my Cindy passed
She'd take a bite of me
Chorus

Peaches in the summer
Apples in the fall
If I can't have the girl I want
I won't have none at all
Chorus

When you go a-fishing
Fish with a hook and line
When you go to marry
Don't ever look behind
Chorus

Columbus Stockade Blues

Way down in Columbus Stockade
Left me there to lose my mind
Thinkin' about my blue-eyed Sally
Pretty little gal that I left behind
Go and leave me if you want to
Never let me cross your mind
In your heart you still love another
Leave me darlin' I don't mind

Last night while I was sleeping
I dreamed that I was in your arms
When I woke I was mistaken
I was peeping through the bars
Go and leave me if you want to
Never let me cross your mind
In your heart you still love another
Leave me darlin' I don't mind

Cotton-Eyed Joe (Old-Time Version)

Play it fast or play it slow
Don't play nothing but Cotton-Eyed Joe
Chorus

Cotton-Eyed Joe is a fine old man
Washed his face in a frying pan
Chorus

Went to the window, went to the door
Couldn't see nothing but Cotton-Eyed Joe
Chorus

Got me a fiddle and a shoe-string bow
Gonna play a tune called Cotton-Eyed Joe
Chorus

Cotton-Eyed Joe (Western Swing Version)

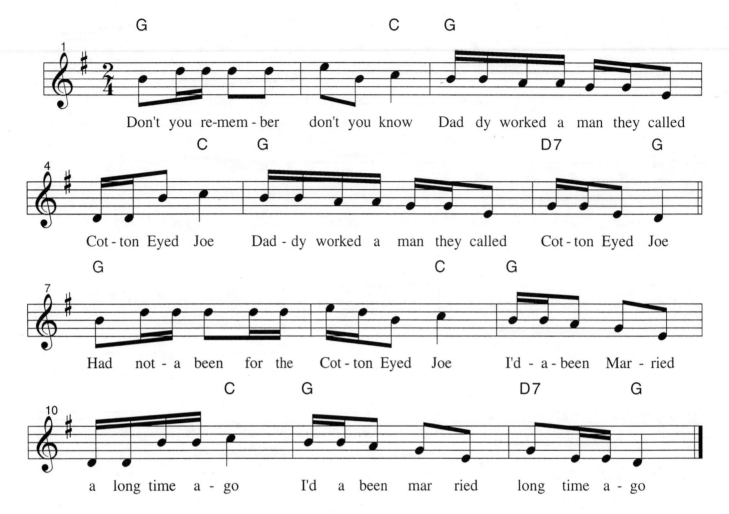

I know a girl, lives down below
Used to go see her but I don't no more
Used to go see her but I don't no more
Chorus

Down in the cotton patch, down below
Everybody's singing the Cotton-Eyed Joe
Everybody's singing the Cotton-Eyed Joe
Chorus

I fell down and I stubbed my toe
Called for the doctor, Cotton-Eyed Joe
Called for the doctor, Cotton-Eyed Joe
Chorus

Tune my fiddle and rosin my bow
Gonna make music everywhere I go
Gonna play a tune called the Cotton-Eyed Joe
Chorus

Crawdad

Now you get the line and I'll get the pole ho-ney
You get the line and I'll get the pole babe You get the line and I'll get the pole
We'll go down to that craw-dad hole Ho-ney ba - by mine

Sat on the bank `til my feet got cold, honey
Sat on the bank `til my feet got cold, babe
Sat on the bank `til my feet got cold
And I'll sit right here `til I grow old honey, baby, mine
Chorus

Yonder come a man with a sack on his back, uh huh
Yonder come a man with a sack on his back, uh huh
Yonder come a man with a sack on his back
Dropped four crawdads and took `em back honey, baby, mine
Chorus

Now he fell down and he busted that sack, honey
Now he fell down and he busted that sack, babe
Now he fell down and he busted that sack
Lost all the crawdads he had packed honey, baby, mine
Chorus

What did the hen duck say to the drake, honey
What did the hen duck say to the drake, babe
What did the hen duck say to the drake
Well there ain't no crawdads in that lake, honey, baby mine
Chorus

25

Cripple Creek

Choruses (sung over "B" strain):

Goin' down to Cripple Creek, goin' in a run
Goin' down to Cripple Creek to have a little fun
Goin' down to Cripple Creek, goin' in a run
Goin' down to Cripple Creek to have a little fun

Roll my britches to my knees
Wade in Cripple Creek if I please
Roll my britches to my knees
Wade in Cripple Creek if I please

Goin' down to Cripple Creek, fast as I can go
Goin' down to Cripple Creek, don't be slow
Goin' down to Cripple Creek, fast as I can go
Goin' down to Cripple Creek, don't be slow

Croquet Habit

Well the cro - quet ha - bit is migh-ty bad But these old ha - bits I've al - ways had Oh hey ho - ney can't you come out to - night

Well way down yonder in the sunny South
Where the sun shines warm in my honey's house
Oh, hey, honey ain't you comin' out tonight

I see my honey goin' across the field
She's winding and twisting like an automobile
Oh, hey, honey don't deny your name

Well I got a woman who lives in town
And when I'm gone she wears a mourning gown
Oh, hey, honey can't you come out tonight

You got a nickel and I got a dime
If you don't mind it'll all be mine
Oh, hey, honey ain't you comin' out tonight

Cry Holy Unto the Lord

Cry holy unto the Lord
Cry holy unto the Lord
In that day when the bells don't toll
Cry holy unto the Lord
Chorus

Sinners run unto the Lord
Sinners run unto the Lord
Now please don't let this harvest pass
And lose your soul at last
Chorus

Cry holy unto the Lord
Cry holy unto the Lord
The four and twenty elders bowing all around the altar
Crying holy unto the Lord
Chorus

The Cuckoo

Gon - na build me a log ca - bin On the moun - tain so high So
I can see Wil - lie As he goes wal - kin' by Oh the
cuck - oo she's a pret - ty bird And she war - bles as she flies She'll
ne - ver say cuck - oo `Til the fourth day of Ju - ly

Well I've played cards in Old England
And I've gambled over in Spain
And I'll bet you ten dollars
That I beat you next Game
Chorus

My horse is dead hungry
And he won't eat your hay
I'll drive on just a little further
Wonderin' why you treat me this way
Chorus

There's one thing that's been a puzzle
Since the day that time began
A man's love for his woman
And her sweet love for her man
Chorus

Devilish Mary

When I was young and fool-ish I thought I ne-ver would mar-ry
Fell in love with a pret-ty lit-tle gal And sure `nough we got mar-ried
Ring dum-ma ding dum da-ry The pret-ti-est gal I
e-ver did see And her name is De-vil-ish Ma-ry

We both were young and foolish
She was just a girlie
We both agreed upon one word
Our wedding day was Thursday
Chorus

We'd been married but two weeks
When she got mean as the devil
Every time I looked at her
She hit me in the head with a shovel
Chorus

She washed my clothes in old soap suds
The back's all filled with stitches
She let me know right from the start
She's gonna wear my britches
Chorus

If I marry another time
Gonna be for love not riches
Marry me a gal `bout two feet high
So she can wear my britches
Chorus

Don't Grieve After Me

We are climbing Jacob's ladder don't you grieve after me (3 times)
Lord I don't want you to grieve after me
Chorus

We will climb it up to heaven don't you grieve after me (3 times)
Lord I don't want you to grieve after me
Chorus

We are going to see our mother don't you grieve after me (3 times)
Lord I don't want you to grieve after me
Chorus

There we'll sing and shout forever don't you grieve after me (3 times)
Lord I don't want you to grieve after me
Chorus

Chorus

Don't Let the Deal Go Down (Texas Fiddle Tune)

Don't Let Your Deal Go Down (Old-Time Song)

Now I been all a-round this whole wide world

Way down to Mem-phis Ten-nes-see

A - ny old place I hang my hat

Looks like home to me

Now I left my little girl a-crying at home
Standing in the door
She threw her little arms around my neck
Saying honey don't you go

I've been all around this whole wide world
Done most every thing
I've played cards with the king and queen
The face card, ace and the ten
Boys, don't let your deal go down
Don't let your deal go down
Don't let your deal go down
For my last old dollar's gone

Where did you get them high-topped shoes
And that dress you wear so fine
Got my shoes from a railroad man
And my dress from a driver in the mines
Chorus

Who's gonna shoe your pretty white feet
Who's gonna glove your hand
Who's gonna kiss your lily white cheeks
Who's gonna be your man

Pappa's gonna shoe my pretty white feet
Mamma's gonna glove my hand
She can kiss my lily white cheeks
`Til you come back again
Chorus

Dreamy Eyes Waltz

Drunkard's Blues

I stepped into the barroom
To get me a drink of gin
Next thing I knew I was reeling
Rocking and drunk again

Chorus:
Whoa, whoa, whoa
Whoa, whoa, whoa
Hey, hey, oh oh oh
Got the Drunkard's Blues

I stumbled onto the sidewalk
Began walking around
I looked everywhere I thought she'd be
But my baby was nowhere around
Chorus

Sixteen coal black horses
All hitched up in line
In that pretty buggy she's riding
Goodbye, old gal of mine
Chorus

Eighth of January

Fiddler's Reel

Fifteen Cents

I left my home in Ten - nes - see I thought I'd learn to tra - vel But I
fell in love with a pret - ty lit - tle girl and then I played the de - vil I
loved that girl and she loved me I thought we'd live to - ge - ther But
then we tied that fa - tal knot and now I'm gone for - e - ver
Give me back my fif - teen cents give me back my mo - ney
Give me back my fif - teen cents and I'll go home to Mam - my

'Twas fifteen cents for the preacher man and a dollar for the paper
Then dear old mother-in-law moved in and Lord it was a caper
I fiddled a tune for her one day and she called me a joker
Then that old sow got mad at me and hit me with a poker
Chorus

I worked in town and I worked on the farm, but there's no way to suit 'em
They're both so dadburn mean to me somebody ought to shoot 'em
I'm tired of looking at my mother-in-law, I'd like to see my granny
So give me back my fifteen cents and I'll go home to mammy
Chorus

Fire on the Mountain

Fisher's Hornpipe

Foggy Mountain Top

If I'd a-listened to what mama said
I would not be here today
Just sitting here in this cold jailhouse
Crying my whole life away
Chorus

Now if you see that girl or mine
There's something you must tell her
She need not waste her precious time
Courting with some other feller
Chorus

She's caused me to weep, she's caused me to mourn
She's caused me to leave my home
Those lonesome pines and the good old times
I'm on my way back home
Chorus

Ginseng Blues

My home ain't here now
It's down in Caroline
I got to killin' down in Georgia
But they swang my dear sweet mama
You can't read my mind
When you think I'm a-lovin' you mama
That's when you oughta cry
(Yodel)

I got a gal down in Georgia
One in Dixie too
If you treat me mean sweet mama
I'll turn my back on you good baby
You can't read my mind
When you think I'm a-lovin' you mama
That's when you oughta cry
(Yodel)

Ain't gonna work on the river
Ain't gonna load no boat
Put my head out the window
Won't you come home sweet mama
You can't read my mind
When you think I'm a-lovin' you mama
That's when you oughta cry
(Yodel)

The Girl I left Behind

Glory to the Lamb

If you want to be real happy, I'll tell you what to do
Just count on Jesus right away, get saved through and through
Go on your way rejoicing, live happy every day
Give God your heart and make the start upon the narrow way
Chorus

On Monday I'm happy, on Tuesday full of joy
On Wednesday I have peace with him that the devil can't destroy
On Thursday, on Friday, I'm walking in the light
And Saturday's a heavenly blue and Sunday's always bright
Chorus

Chorus

Great Big Taters

End with first strain

Groundhog

Yonder comes Molly with a ten-foot pole
Yonder comes Molly with a ten-foot pole
Twist this whistle-pig out of its hole
Oh groundhog

Come here boys, come here quick
Come here boys, come here quick
This old goundhog's made me sick
Oh groundhog

Yonder comes Molly with a smile and a grin
Yonder comes Molly with a smile and a grin
Groundhog gravy all over her chin
Oh groundhog

Yonder comes granny walkin' on a cane
Yonder comes granny walkin' on a cane
Swore she'd eat those groundhog brains
Oh groundhog

Here comes Molly with a ten-foot pole
Here comes Molly with a ten-foot pole
We're gettin this groundhog out of its hole
Oh groundhog

Ham Beats All Meat

While you're in the dining room
Eating on mutton and lamb
I'll be in the kitchen
Goin' for that good sweet ham
Chorus (sing twice)

Haste to the Wedding Quadrille

He Rambled

My mo-ther raised three grown sons Bus-ter Bill and I

Bus - ter was the black sheep of our lit-tle fa-mi-ly

Mo-ther tried to break him of his rough and row-dy ways

Fin-`ly had to get the judge to give him nine-ty days And did-n't he

ram - ble Ram - ble

Ram-ble all a - round In and out of town And did-n't he

ram - ble Ram - ble He

ram-bled `til the but-chers cut him down

He rambled in a gambling game, he gambled on the green
The gamblers there showed him a trick that he had never seen
He lost his roll in Zurich and he almost lost his life
He lost the car that carried him there and somebody stole his wife
Chorus

He rambled to a swell hotel, his appetite was stout
When he refused to pay the bill the landlord threw him out
He raised a brick to smack him with and when he wouldn't stop
The landlord kicked him o'er the fence right in a barrel of slop
Chorus

Hesitation Blues

I'm stan - ding on the cor - ner with a dol - lar in my hand Just
loo - king for a wo - man who's a - loo - king for a man Now
I'm not the doc - tor just the doc - tor's son But
I can do the doc - tor `til the doc - tor comes Tell me
how long do I have to wait? Can I get you
now? Or must I hes - i - tate?

I've got a woman and a sweetheart too
My woman don't love me but my sweetheart do
She only likes two kind-a men I'm told
She likes 'em young and she likes 'em old
Tell me how long do I have to wait?
Can I get you now, or must I hesitate?

If the river was whiskey and the banks were wine
You'd see me wading just any old time
If the river was whiskey and I was a duck
I'd dive to the bottom and I'd never comes up
Tell me how long do I have to wait?
Can I get you now, or must I hesitate?

I was born in England, raised in France
Bought a suit of clothes and they wouldn't send the pants
I was born in Alabama, raised in Tennessee
If you don't like my peaches, don't shake my tree
Tell me how long do I have to wait?
Can I get you now, or must I hesitate?

I looked down the road just as far as I could see
A man had my woman and the blues had me
Got the hesitating stockings and the hesitation shoes
And a hesitating mama that I can't afford to lose
Tell me how long do I have to wait?
Can I get you now, or must I hesitate?

A sixteen-bar arrangement of this tune has become standard among contemporary players. If you prefer the twelve-bar version as recorded by Charlie Poole, Milton Brown and others, use two lines of each verse and then go to the chorus.

Hills of Roane County

In the beau-ti - ful hills

Way back in Roane Coun-ty

That's where I have roamed for ma-ny long years

That's where my heart Was bro-ken for-e-ver

That's where the first step of mis-for-tune I made

I was thirty years old
When I courted and married
Amanda Gilbreath I then called my wife
Her brother stabbed me
For some unknown reason
Just three months later I'd taken Tom's life

For twenty-six years
This world I have rambled
I've been to England to France and to Spain
I thought of my home
Way back in Roane County
I boarded a steamer and came home again

I was captured and tried
In the village of Kingston
Not a man in that county would speak one kind word
When the jury came in
With the verdict next morning
A lifetime in prison were the words that I heard

When the train pulled out
Poor mother stood weeping
And sister sat there all alone with a sigh
The last words I heard
Were Willie God bless you
Willie God bless you, God bless you goodbye

No matter what happened
To me in Roane County
No matter how long my sentence may be
I love my old home
Way back in Roane County
It's way back down in old East Tennessee

In the scorching hot sun
Of this prison I'm working
Just working and toiling my whole life away
So when you write home
From this prison in Nashville
Place one of my songs in your letter for me

Home on the Range

How Long

Have you seen my baby baby baby, tell her to hurry home
I ain't had no good feeling, how long, how long
And I'm on my way, babe, how long, how long

Now listen to me mama mama mama
Oh Lord now baby, how long, how long
I ain't had no loving, how long, how long

I hate the train train that carried my baby away
And left me standing, how long, how long
I ain't had no loving, how long, how long

I never can forget that day
When you called be baby, how long, how long
I ain't had no loving since my babe's been gone

Now listen baby, baby, everything's all right with me
Oh Lord now baby, how long, how long
I ain't had no loving since my babe's been gone

I Want to Go Where Jesus Is

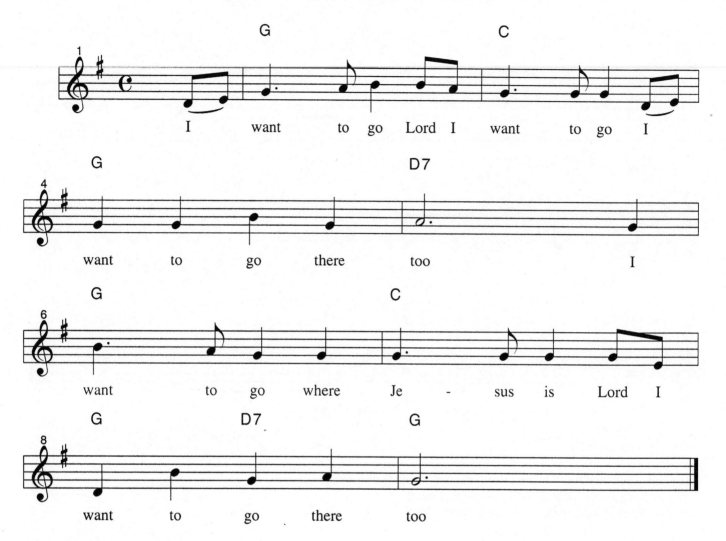

If you get there before I do
Lord I want to go there too
Just look for me, I'm coming through
Lord I want to go there too
Chorus

Our loving mother done gone on
Lord I want to go there too
I promise that I'll follow on
Lord I want to go there too
Chorus

Our loving father done gone on
Lord I want to go there too
I promise that I'll follow on
Lord I want to go there too
Chorus

Chorus

I Wonder If You Feel The Way I Do

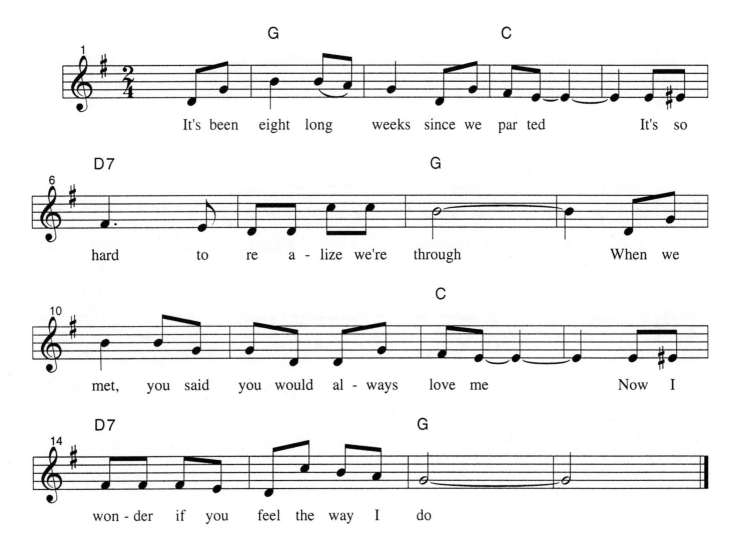

It's been eight long weeks since we par ted It's so
hard to re a - lize we're through When we
met, you said you would al - ways love me Now I
won - der if you feel the way I do

I'll ne'er forget our days together
Even though we know they're very few
I loved you then and will forever
I wonder if you feel the way I do

It's the strangest and the sweetest love, dear
That two people ever knew
You told me that I need not worry
That forever you'd be true

It makes no difference where I wander
No matter what I say or do
I'll always think of you my darling
And I wonder if you feel the way I do

59

Ida Red

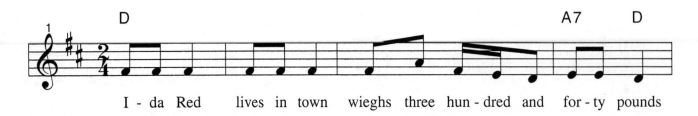

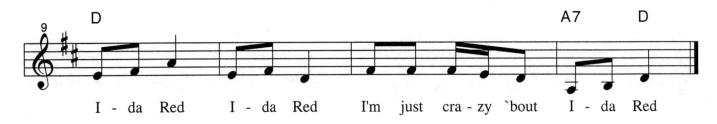

Down the road, far as I can see
See them pretty girls looking at me
Down the road about a mile and a half
Can't see my honey but I hear her laugh
Chorus

Going into town with my hat in my hand
Hello, sherrif I've killed my man
Ida Red Working on the road
Working off the money to pay our board
Chorus

Ida Red, Ida Blue
I got stuck on Ida too
Bought me a horse, fixed me a sled
Nobody's gonna ride but Ida Red
Chorus

I'm A Man of Constant Sorrow

With generous rubato

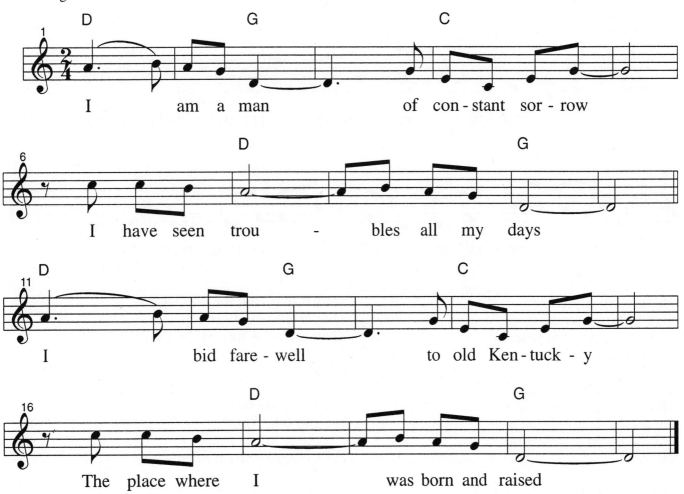

I am a man of con-stant sor-row

I have seen trou - bles all my days

I bid fare - well to old Ken-tuck - y

The place where I was born and raised

Oh, for six long years I've been in trouble
My pleasure here on earth is done
For in this world, I have to ramble
I have no friends to help me now

Oh, fare you well, my own true lover
I fear I'll never see you again
For I am bound to ride the Northern Railroad
Perhaps I'll die upon the train

Oh, you can bury me in some deep valley
For many years, where I may lay
And while you're dreaming, while you're slumbering
While I am sleeping in the clay

Oh, its fare you well to my native country
The place where I have loved so well
For I have had all kinds of trouble
In this vain world, no tongue can tell

But friends although I may be a stranger
My face you may never see no more
But there's one promise that can be given
Where we can meet upon that beautiful shore

61

I'm Troubled

I'm trou-bled I'm trou-bled I'm trou-bled in mind If

trou-ble don't kill me I'll live a long time

Oh meeting is pleasure
And parting is grief
And a false-hearted woman
Is worse than a thief

A thief can but rob you
And take what you save
But a false-hearted true love
Will take you to your grave
Chorus

The grave will decay you
And turn you to dust
There ain't a girl in a million
A poor boy can trust

They'll hug you, they'll kiss you
They'll tell you more lies
Than the cross ties on the railroad
Or the stars in the sky
Chorus

I'm going to Georgia
I'm going to Rome
I'm going to Georgia
For to make it my home

I'll build me a cabin
On the mountain so high
Where the wild birds and the whipoorwills
Can hear my sad cry
Chorus

Johnny Lover

Jessie James

It was on a moonlight night
The stars were shining bright
They robbed the Glendale train
And the people they did say
For many miles away
It was robbed by Frank and Jesse James
Chorus

It was old Robert Ford
That dirty little coward
I wonder how he does feel
For he ate of Jesse's bread
And slept in Jesse's bed
Then laid Jesse James in his grave
Chorus

People held their breath
When the learned of Jesse's death
They wondered how he'd come to fall
He was shot in the back
By little Robert Ford
While he hung a picture on the wall
Chorus

June Apple

Just a Spoonful

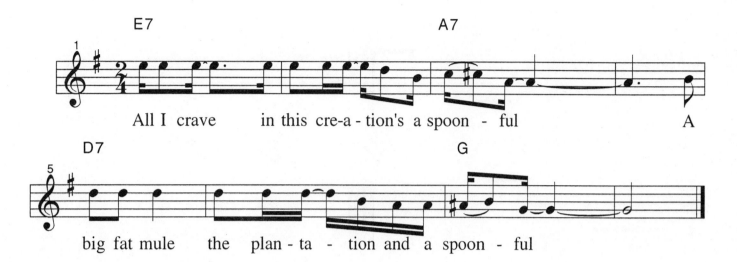

Just a spoonful, just a spoonful
A spoonful, just a spoonful

I'd smack the judge, go to jail for a spoonful
I'd go to jail, don't want to bail for a spoonful

My baby says she couldn't get that spoonful
I said look here gal, don't you fool with me `bout my spoonful

I'd walk the streets all night long looking for my spoonful
My spoonful, for my spoonful

Look here gal, don't you fool with me `bout that spoonful
It's a spoonful, just a spoonful

My baby cried all night long for a spoonful
She thought she wasn't gonna get that doggone spoonful

Police caught me, he knocked me down for a spoonful
I caught the train, I left this town for a spoonful

Katy Cline

I wish I was a little bird
I would not build my nest upon the ground
I'd build my nest in the tall willow tree
Where the bad boys could not tear it down
Chorus

Away from my little cabin home
Away from my little cabin home
Where there's no one to weep, no one to mourn
There's no one to be with Katy Cline
Chorus

Oh do you know my Katy Cline
She lives at the foot of the hill
In a quiet little nook by the babbling brook
That runs by her dear old father's fields
Chorus

Keep Knocking But You Can't Come In

Kinda busy so you can't come in
Kinda busy so you can't come in
Kinda busy so you can't come in
Guess you'd better let me be

You've had your chances now you can't come in
Had your chances now you can't come in
Had your chances so you can't come in
Guess you'd better let me be

Shake my doorknob but you can't get in
Shake my doorknob but you can't get in
Shake my doorknob but you can't get in
Guess you'd better let me be

You thought you had me on the rack
That I'd be here when you got back
But I'm running on another track
Guess you'd better let me be

I know you been drinkin' gin
Runnin' `round with other men
Keep knocking but you can't get in
Guess you'd better let me be

Keep bootin' but you can't get in
Busy bootin' so you can't come in
Busy bootin' so you can't come in
Guess you'd better let me be

I'm busy bootin' so you can't come in
You've had your chances now you can't come in
Shake my doorknob now you can't come in
Guess you'd better let me be

L and N Rag

End with first strain

Liberty

Living Where the Healing Waters Flow

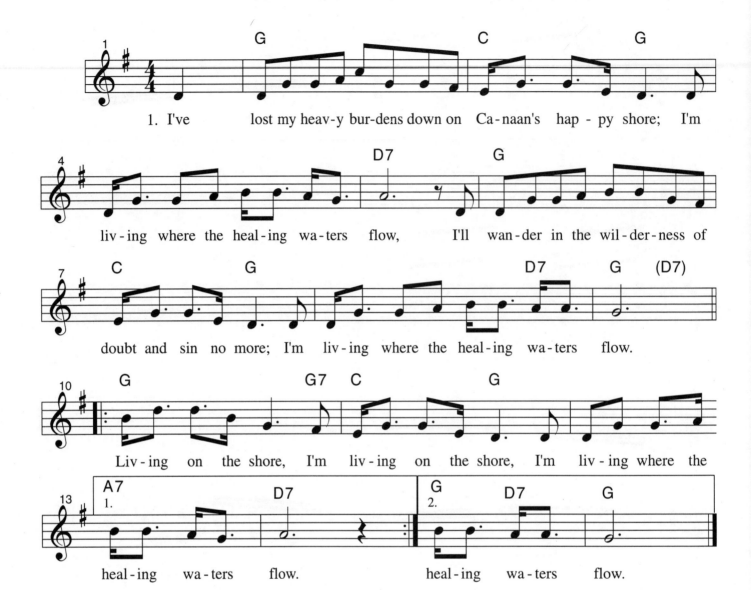

2. With Israel's trusting children,
I'm rejoicing on my way;
I'm living where the healing waters flow.
The cloudy, fiery pillar is my guiding light today;
Chorus

3. My hun-g'ring soul is satisfied,
with manna from above;
I'm living where the healing waters flow.
No more I thirst; the Rock I've found,
That Fount of endless love.
Chorus

4. I'm singing, "Hallelujah";
safely anchored is my soul.
I'm living where the healing waters flow.
I'm resting on His promises;
the Blood has made me whole.
Chorus

CHORUS:
I'm living where the healing waters flow
Living on the shore, I'm living on the shore.
I'm living where the healing waters flow.
healing waters flow.

Lonesome Road Blues
(aka Goin' Down the Road Feelin' Bad)

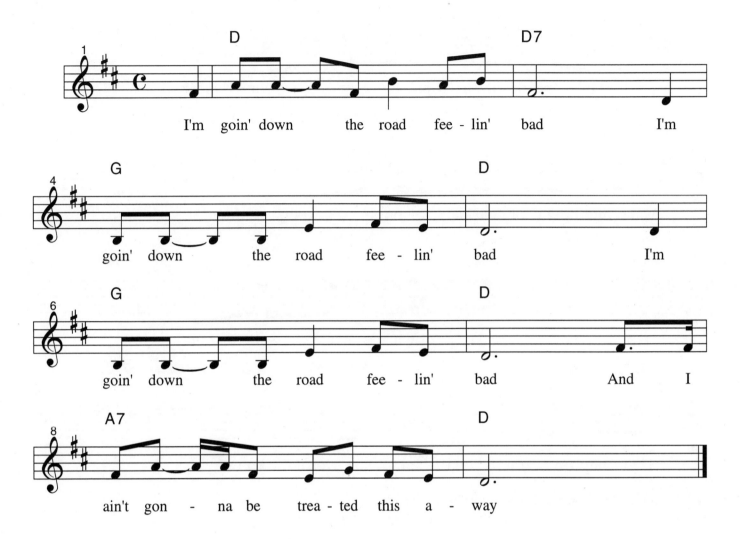

I'm goin' down the road fee-lin' bad I'm
goin' down the road fee-lin' bad I'm
goin' down the road fee-lin' bad And I
ain't gon-na be trea-ted this a-way

I'm goin' where that chilly wind don't blow
I'm goin' where that chilly wind don't blow
Yes I'm goin' where that chilly wind don't blow
And I ain't gonna be treated this a-way

I'm goin' to where the climate suits my clothes
I'm goin' to where the climate suits my clothes
Yes I'm goin' to where the climate suits my clothes
And I ain't gonna be treated this a-way

I don't care if I never do come back
No I don't care if I never do come back
No I don't care if I never do come back
And I ain't gonna be treated this a-way

Make Me a Pallet on the Floor

Don't you let my good gal catch you here (repeat)
Honey, she might shoot you, might cut and stab you too
Ain't no telling just what she might do

I'm going up the country, through the sleet and snow (repeat)
Going up the country, through the sleet and snow
No telling how much further I may go

Eat my breakfast here and my dinner in Tennessee (repeat)
Eat my breakfast here, my dinner in Tennessee
I told you I was coming, baby won't you wait for me

The way I've been sleeping, my back and shoulder's tired (repeat)
The way I've been sleeping, my back and shoulder's tired
Gonna turn over and try it on my side

(Repeat second verse)

Mama Don't Allow

Mama don't allow no banjo playing `round here
Mama don't allow no banjo playing `round here
But I don't care what mama say, gonna play my banjo anyway
Mama don't allow no banjo playing `round here

(Repeat for other instruments)

Maple on the Hill

Near a qui-et coun-try vil-lage grew a ma-ple on a hill As I sat with my be-lo-ved long a-go When the stars were shi-ning bri-ghtly we could hear the whi-poor-will As we sat be-neath the ma-ple on the hill

Chorus:
Don't forget me little darling when they've laid me down to die
Just a little wish darling that I crave
As you linger there in sadness you are thinking of a past
As we sat beneath the maple on the hill

We would sing our songs together when the birds had gone to rest
We would listen to the murmer on the ridge
Will you love me little darling as you did those starry nights
When we sat beneath the maple on the hill
Chorus

I will soon be with the angels on that bright and happy shore
Even now I hear them coming o'er the ridge
It's goodbye my little darling, it is time for us to part
I must leave you at the maple on the hill
Chorus

Midnight on the Stormy Deep

I never shall forget the day
That I was forced to go away
In silence there my head she grasped
And pressed me to her loving breast

Oh Willie don't go back to sea
There's other girls as good as me
But none can love you true as I
Please don't go where the bullets fly

The deep deep sea may us divide
And I may be some other's bride
But still my thoughts may sometimes stray
To thee when thou are far away

I never have proved false to thee
The heart I gave is true as thine
But you have proved untrue to me
I can no longer call you mine

Then fare thee well I'd rather make
My home upon some icy lake
Where the southern sun refuse to shine
Then to trust a love as false as thine

My Home's Across the Blue Ridge Mountains

How can I keep from crying
How can I keep from crying
Tell me how can I keep from crying
When I never expect to see you anymore
Chorus

Love can feed my baby candy
Love can feed my baby candy
Love can feed my baby candy
Oh, I can never expect to see you anymore
Chorus

How can I keep from crying
How can I keep from crying
How can I keep from crying
When I never expect to see you anymore
Chorus

My Wife Died Saturday Night

My wife died Sa-tur-day night Sun-day she was bu-ried

Mon-day was my cour-tin' day and Tues-day I got mar-ried

Fiddle break

Round and round up and down
Every day I wander
Round round up and down
Looking for my honey

(Repeat first verse)

New River Train

Oh darling, you can't love one (repeat)
You can't love one and have any fun
Darling, you can't love one
Chorus

Oh darling, you can't love two (repeat)
You can't love two and have your little heart be true
Oh darling, you can't love two
Chorus

Oh darling, you can't love three (repeat)
You can't love three and still love me
Oh darling, you can't love three
Chorus

Oh darling, you can't love four (repeat)
You can't love four and love me any more
Darling, you can't love four
Chorus

Oh darling, you can't love five (repeat)
You can't love five and get honey from my beehive
Darling, you can't love five
Chorus

Oh darling, you can't love six (repeat)
You can't love six that kind of love won't mix
Oh darling, you can't love six
Chorus

Oh darling, you can't love seven (repeat)
You can't love seven and still get into heaven
Oh darling, you can't love seven
Chorus

Continue *ad infinitum*

Nine-Pound Hammer

I'm going to the mountain
For to see my darlin'
But I ain't coming back
No I ain't coming back
Chorus

Ain't one hammer
In this whole tunnel
That rings like mine
That rings like mine
Chorus

Rings like silver
Sines like gold
Oh it rings like silver
And it shines like gold
Chorus

Somebody stole
My nine-pound hammer
They've took it and gone
They've took it and gone
Chorus

Nine-pound hammer
It killed John Henry
Ain't a-gonna kill me
Ain't a-gonna kill me
Chorus

No Disappointment in Heaven

Nobody's Dirty Business

Ain't no - bo - dy's dir-ty biz - ness how my ba - by treats me

No - bo - dy's biz - ness but mine

Ain't no - bo - dy's dog - gone biz - ness how my ba - by treats me

No-bo - dy's biz-ness but my own

One of these mornings gonna wake up crazy
Grab my gun and kill my baby
Nobody's business but mine
Ain't nobody's doggone business
How my baby treats me
Nobody's business but my own

One of these mornings gonna wake up boozy
Gonna grab my gun, gonna kill old Suzy
Nobody's business but mine
Going back to Pensecola
Gonna buy my babe a money molar
Nobody's business but my own

Say, babe, did you get that letter
Would you take me back, I'll treat you better
Nobody's business but mine
Ain't nobody's doggone business
How my baby treats me
Nobody's business but my own

(Repeat second verse)

(Repeat first verse)

Mississippi John Hurt's 1928 recording uses 7-bar phrases.   *If you prefer this, skip the measure after each dotted barline.*

Oh, Mary Don't Weep

Oh Ma - ry don't you weep don't you mourn

Oh Ma - ry don't you weep don't you mourn Pha - raoh's ar - my got

drown - ded Oh Ma - ry don't weep

If I could, I surely would
Stand on the rock where Moses stood
Pharaoh's army got drownded
Oh, Mary don't weep
Chorus

Mary weeped, Martha mourned
All around God's holy throne
Pharaoh's army got drownded
Oh, Mary don't weep
Chorus

God told Moses by the rainbow sign
No more water but fire next time
Pharaoh's army got drownded
Oh, Mary don't weep
Chorus

I told you once and I told you twice
You can't get to heaven with a sweetheart and a wife
Pharaoh's army got drownded
Oh, Mary don't weep
Chorus

One of these days about twelve o'clock
This old world's gonna reel and rock
Pharaoh's army got drownded
Oh, Mary don't weep
Chorus

Old Joe Clark

Oozlin' Daddy Blues

I went to get my fot-tune told Gave the gal my hand to hold

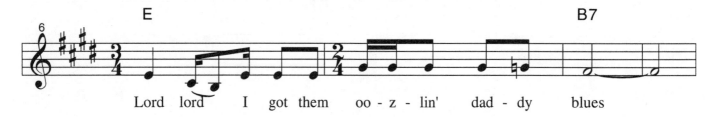

Lord lord I got them oo-z-lin' dad-dy blues

It was in a gyp-sy place she read my mind and slapped my face

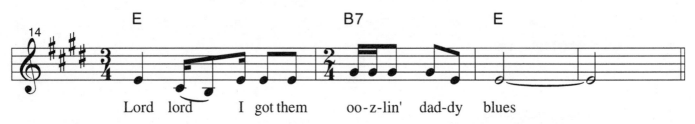

Lord lord I got them oo-z-lin' dad-dy blues

Yo-de-lee-o-le-hee yo-de-lee-o-le-hee le-hee O-e-o-o

Two old maids in a folding bed
One turned over and the other one said
Lord, lord, got them oozlin' daddy blues
Two old men in a great big row
One caught the other one a-lovin' his cow
Lord, lord, got them oozlin' daddy blues
(Yodel)

I know the lawyers will be by
Lord they all know how to lie
Lord, lord, got them oozlin' daddy blues
But the preacher man, he's the worst of all
He'll preach and preach his salary's too small
Lord, lord, got them oozlin' daddy blues
(Yodel)

I got a gal from Mexico
She can oozle easy, fast or slow
Lord, lord, got them oozlin' daddy blues
If she don't let my oozler be
They're gonna have to lay a lilly on me
Lord, lord, got them oozlin' daddy blues
(Yodel)

Whiskey, women, wine and song
I know that they've led me wrong
Lord, lord, got them oozlin' daddy blues
Gonna quit drinkin', change my life
Land me a flapper for my wife
Lord, lord, got them oozlin' daddy blues
(Yodel)

Pass Around the Bottle

Pass a - round the bot - tle and we'll all take a drink

Pass a - round the bot - tle and we'll all take a drink

Pass a - round the bot - tle and we'll all take a drink As

we go mar - ching on

Chorus:
Glory, glory to old Georgia
Glory, glory to old Georgia
Glory, glory to old georgia
As we go marching on

Hang Jeff Davis from a sour apple tree
Hang Jeff Davis from a sour apple tree
Hang Jeff Davis from a sour apple tree
As we go marching by
Chorus

Old Aunt Peggy, won't you fill `em up again
Old Aunt Peggy, won't you fill `em up again
Old Aunt Peggy, won't you fill `em up again
As we go marching on
Chorus

Chorus

Pick Poor Robin Clean

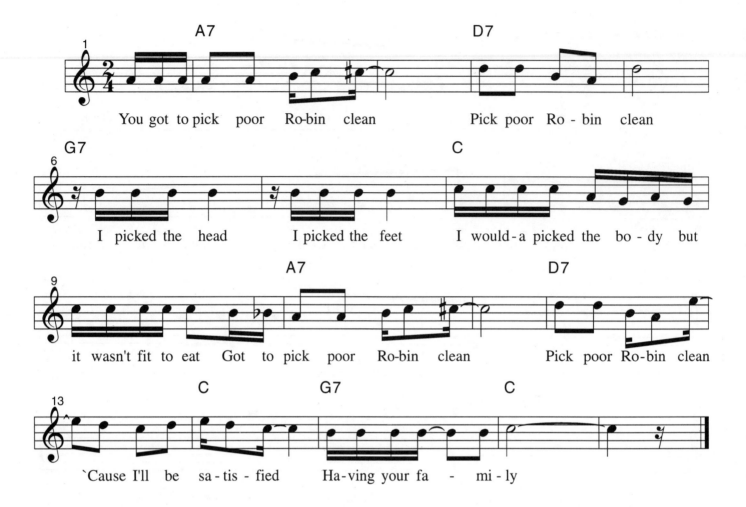

Get off my money, now don't get funny
`Cause I'm a rounder, don't catch no flounder
Gambling for Sadie, she is my lady
I'm a hustling fool, that's just what I am
Chorus

Oh didn't that jaybird laugh, when he picked poor Robin clean
Picked poor Robin clean, picked poor Robin clean
Didn't that jaybird laugh, when he picked poor Robin clean
`Cause I'll be satisfied, having your family
Chorus

Red River Valley

Chorus:
Come and sit by my side if you love me
Do not hasten to bid me adieu
But remember the Red River Valley
And the one that has loved you so true

For a long time I've waited, my darling
For those words that you never would say
But alas all my fond hopes have vanished
For they say you are going away
Chorus

Won't you think of the valley you're leaving
Oh, how lonely and sad it will be
Won't you think of the kind heart you're breaking
And the pain you are causing to me
Chorus

I have promised you darling that never
Would a word from my lips cause you pain
And my life it will be yours forever
If you only will love me again
Chorus

Oh there never could be such a longing
In the heart of a pure maiden's breast
Than dwells in the heart you are breaking
As I wait in my home in the west
Chorus

As you go to your home by the ocean
May you never forget those sweet hours
That we spent in the Red River Valley
And the love we exchanged amid the flowers
Chorus

Ragged But Right

I tell all you peo - ple I'm rag-ged but right I'm a

thief and a gam - bler I get drunk e - v'ry night Eat a

por - ter - house steak three times a day for my board It's

more than a - ny loa - fer in this town can af - ford

Big e - lec - tric fan to keep me cool while I sleep

Lil' ba - by girl to play a - round at my feet I'm a

Rank Strangers to Me

I wan-dered a-gain to my home in the
They've all moved a-way said the voice of a

moun-tains where in life's ear-ly dawn
stran-ger To a beau-ti-ful home

I was hap-py and free I looked for my
By the bright crys-tal sea Some beau-ti-ful

friends But I ne-ver could find them
day I will meet them in hea-ven

I found they were all Rank stran-gers to
Where no one will be A stran-ger to

me
me E-`vry bo-dy I met

Roll 'Em on the Ground

Roll 'em boys rolll 'em Roll 'em on the ground

Shoot that se-ven e - le - ven Roll 'em all a - round

When she sees me coming
She lifts her head and smiles
When she sees me leaving
She hangs her head and cries
Chorus

I don't think she likes me
Because I'm rough and rowdy
Every time I see that gal
She hardly tells me howdy
Chorus

I went to kiss my gal last night
Her love I was a-seeking
Missed her mouth and kissed her nose
The gosh durn thing was leaking
Chorus

Chorus

Roll In My Sweet Baby's Arms

Ain't gon - na work on the rail - road
Ain't gon - na work on the farm Well I'll
lay `round the shack `til the mail train comes back Then I'll
roll in my sweet ba - by's arms

Chorus:
Roll in my sweet baby's arms
Roll in my sweet baby's arms
Gonna lay round the shack `til the mailtrain comes back
Then I'll roll in my sweet baby's arms

Sometimes threre's a change in the ocean
Sometimes there's a change in the sea
Somtimes there's a change in my own true love
But there's never a change in me
Chorus

They tell me your parents don't like me
They drove me away from your door
If I had my time to do over, Lord
I'd never go there any more
Chorus

Mamma's a ginger cake baker
Sister can weave and can spin
Daddy's got an interest in that old cotton mill
Just watch that cotton roll in
Chorus

Where were you last Friday night
When I was down in jail
Walking the streets with another man
Wouldn't even throw my bail
Chorus

Saint Anne's Reel

Salt River

Saro

Sa - ro in the moun - tains   And Sa - ro in the seas
going   to see my Sa - ro   My lit-tle old Sa - ro Jane

When she sees me coming
She wrings her hands and sighs
Yonder somes the sweetest thing
That ever lived or died

She hugged me and she kissed me
She called me sugar plum
She threw her arms around me
And I knew my time had come

She took me in the parlor
She cooled me with her fan
She whispered Lord, oh Mamma dear,
I love that dark-eyed man

Come and love me Saro
Say that you'll be mine
You shall be my lady
As long as sun shall shine

I wish I had a nickel
I wish I had a dime
I wish I had a pretty little girl
To kiss and call her mine

Rings upon her fingers
Are shining finest gold
Going to see my Saro
Before she gets too old

Shady Grove

Once I had a fortune
I laid it in a trunk
Lost it all a-gambling
One night when I got drunk

If I had a needle and thread
Fine as I could sew
I'd sew my sweetheart to my side
And down the road I'd go

Cross that mountain one more time
And if I still can't find you
Swing your partner one last time
And grab that gal behind you

It's dark every day and Sunday too
Seems so dark and hazy
Thinking about my Shady Grove
She darn near drove me crazy

Suggested form: chorus/ verse/ chorus/ instrumental break

Shady Grove (Modal Version)

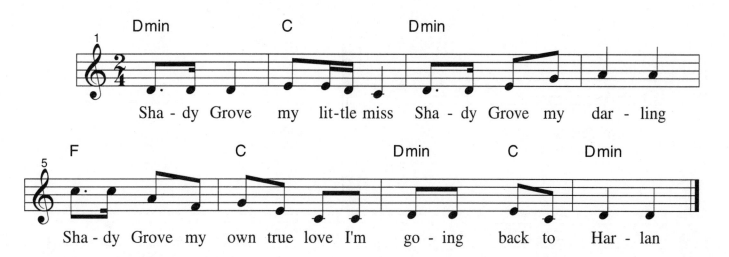

Sha - dy Grove my lit-tle miss Sha - dy Grove my dar - ling

Sha - dy Grove my own true love I'm go - ing back to Har - lan

Shady Grove, my little love
She was standing in the door
Her shoes and stockings in her hands
Her little bare feet on the floor

I wish I had a big fine horse
And the corn to feed him on
Pretty little woman to stay at home
And feed him when I'm gone
Chorus

Cheeks as red as a blooming rose
Eyes of the prettiest brown
She's the darling of my heart
The prettiest girl in town

A kiss from little Shady Grove
As sweet as brandy wine
There ain't no girl in this whole world
Who's prettier than mine
Chorus

Sleep, Baby Sleep

Sleep,   ba - by   sleep - y

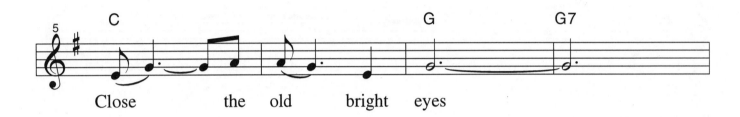

Close   the old   bright   eyes

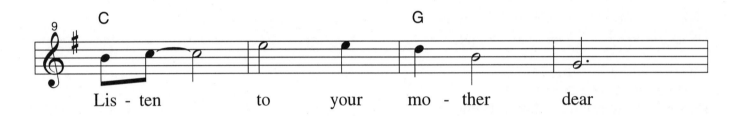

Lis - ten   to   your   mo - ther   dear

Sing   these lul - la - bies

Sleep, baby, sleepy
While angels watch over you
Listen to your mother dear
While she sings for you

(Repeat second verse)

(Yodel)

Soldier's Joy

Verse (sung over "A" strain):
I'm a-goin' to get a drink, don't you want to go
I'm a-goin' to get a drink, don't you want to go
I'm a-goin' to get a drink, don't you want to go
Oh, that Soldier's Joy

Somewhere in Tennessee

Some - where in Ten - nes - see   O - ver the dis - tant hills

Some - one's a - wai - ting me   Her emp - ty arms   to   fill

She's   knee - ling down to pray   While   I   am   drif - ting a - way

An - gels re - peat to me   Son be   not   a - fraid

Somewhere in Tennessee
Out on the road tonight
I sing a song of grief
Trying my tears to dry
Still I can hear her pray
Send me an angel brave
With love protecting me
Knowing I'm yet unsaved

Somewhere in Tennessee
Sad and yearning tonight
I hear her tender plea
Break through the still of the night
While others sleep in peace
She's by her window awake
Through tears of lonely grief
Watching the path to the grave

Somewhere in Tennessee
Angels will tell her tonight
That God has made me free
Heeding my sinful cries
And o'er the sea of death
Safe from the stealing waves
I'll join her soul at rest
Somewhere beyond the grave

Sourwood Mountain

Sourwood Mountain also sounds nice in "F."

Stack-O-Lee Blues

Bill Lyons says to Stack-O-Lee, won't you spare my life
I've got two little babes and a darling loving wife
That bad man, oh cruel Stack-O-Lee

What do I care about your two little babes and your darling loving wife
You've done stole my Stetson hat and I'm bound to take your life
`Cause I'm a bad man, they call me Stack-O-Lee

Boom boom, boom boom, with a forty-four
And when I spied Billy Lyons he was lying on the floor
That bad man, oh cruel Stack-O-Lee

Gentlemen of the jury, what do you think of that
Stack-O-Lee killed Bill Lyons `bout a five-dollar Stetson hat
That bad man, oh cruel Stack-O-Lee

Standing on the gallows, his head way up high
At twelve o`clock they hung him, we were all glad to see him die
That bad man, oh cruel Stack-O-Lee

Sweet Sunny South

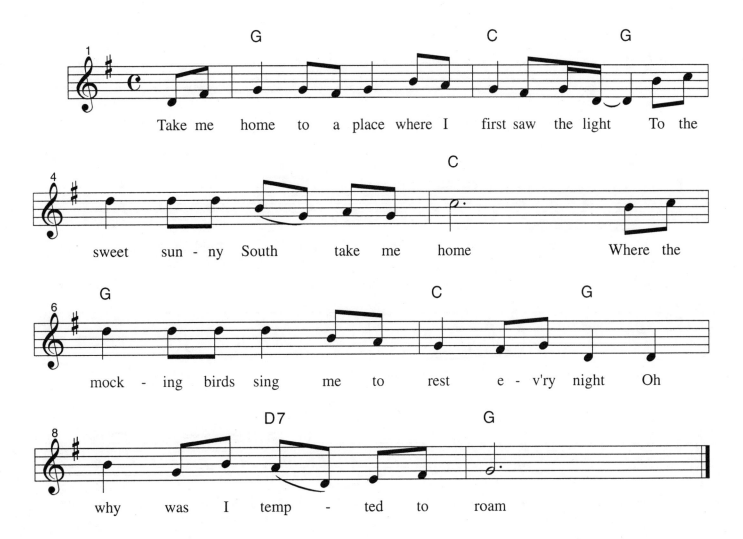

Take me home to a place where I first saw the light To the
sweet sun - ny South take me home Where the
mock - ing birds sing me to rest e - v'ry night Oh
why was I temp - ted to roam

Oh I think with regret of the dear home I left
And the warm hearts that sheltered me there
Of the wife and the dear ones of whom I bereft
And the sight of the old place again

Take me home to a place where my little ones sleep
And old ma she lies dead nearby
Oh the graves of the loved ones I long had to weep
Among them to rest and to die

The path to our cottage they say has grown free
And the place is quite lonely around
And I know that the smiles of the friends I have seen
Now lie in the cold mossy ground

But yet I return to the place of my birth
Where the children have played `round the door
Where they gathered wildflowers to place by the hearth
They will echo our footsteps no more

Take A Drink On Me

Keep on stalling, you'll make me think
Your daddy was a monkey and your mama was an ape
Oh, Lord, honey take a drink on me
Chorus

See that gal with the bonnet on
She's good looking, just as sure as you're born
Oh, Lord, honey take a drink on me
Chorus

(Repeat verses)

Tear It Down (Bed Slats and All)

Now to bake them biscuits nice and brown
You know by god you gotta burn the house down
I got a gal she's little and low
She used to let me shake it but she don't no more
And if I catch another mule kickin' in my stall, I'm a-gonna tear it down
Chorus

Now you can drink your whiskey and have your fun
And run like hell when the policeman comes
Goin' down to the river take a rocking chair
If the blues overtake me I'll rock away from there
And if I catch another mule kickin' in my stall, I'm a-gonna tear it down
Chorus

I had a gal, her name was Bernice
Everytime I slapped her she would holler police
Goin' down to the river, lay my head down
If the blues overtake me I'll jump in and drown
And if I catch another mule kickin' in my stall, I'm a-gonna tear it down
Chorus

Texas Hambone Blues

Oh the blues ain't no - thin' oh the blues ain't no - thin' but a
good man fee - lin' bad Oh the blues ain't no - thin' but a
good man fee - lin' bad Those
must - `ve been the kind of blues I had

Oh yonder come, oh yonder come a train comin' down the track
Oh yonder come a train comin' down the track
Gonna take me away but it's never gonna bring me back

I'm goin' back to Cowtown, goin' to Cowtown to get my hambone boiled
Goin' down to Cowtown to get my hambone boiled
`Cause the New York women done let my hambone spoil

Oh when I die, oh when I die, honey don't you wear no black
Oh when I die, honey don't you wear no black
`Cause if you do, my ghost'll come sneakin' back

Got a gal in Houston, got a gal in Houston, got a gal in San Antone
Got a gal in Houston, got a gal in San Antone
But my Dallas gal'll make a good man leave his home

Got a red-headed woman, got a red-headed woman, make a hound dog lose his trail
Got a red-headed woman make a hound dog lose his trail
Got a black-haired woman make a tadpole hug a whale

Texas Quickstep

There's a Brownskin Gal Down the Road Somewhere

The Titanic

When they were building the Titanic, they said what they could do
They were going to build a ship that the water could not go through
But God with his mighty hand told the world it cannot stand
It was sad when that great ship went down
Chorus

When ship left the land, they were making for the shore
The rich they declared they would not ride with the poor
So they sent the poor below, they were the first to go
It was sad when that great ship went down
Chorus

When the people on the ship were a long way from home
With friends all around them, didn't know their time had come
But death came riding by, sixteen hundred had to die
It was sad when that great ship went down
Chorus

Tom Cat Blues

Ring-Tailed Tom on the fence
The old pussy cat on the ground
Ring-Tailed Tom come off-a that fence
And they went round and around

Lord he's quick on the trigger
He's a natural-born quick shot
He finds a new target every night
And he sure does practice a lot
(Yodel)

He makes them roust about
He makes them roll their eyes
They can't resist my Ring-Tailed Tom
No matter how they try

You better watch old Ring-Tailed Tom
He's boss around the town
He won't have a pussy cat
Tom-cattin' around
(Yodel)

Ring-Tailed Tom is a stud
He struts around the town
All the pussy cats in the neighborhood
Can't get old Ring-Tail down

He's always runnin' around
Just can't be satisfied
He goes out every night
With a new one by his side
(Yodel)

Turkey in the Straw

Two Dollar Bill
(aka My Long Journey Home)

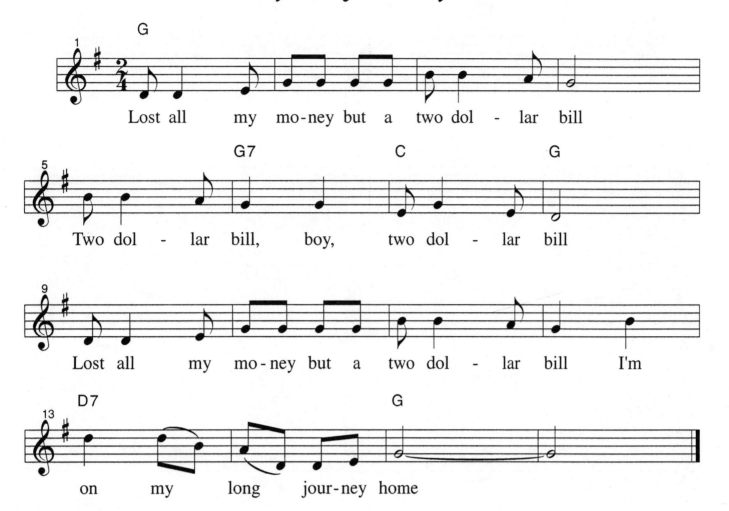

Lost all my mo-ney but a two dol-lar bill
Two dol-lar bill, boy, two dol-lar bill
Lost all my mo-ney but a two dol-lar bill I'm
on my long jour-ney home

Black smoke's a-rising, it surely is a train
Surely is a train, boy, surely is a train
Black smoke's a-rising, it surely is a train
I'm on my long journey home

All sick and lonely and I'm feeling kind of blue
Feeling kind of blue, boy, feeling kind of blue
All sick and lonely and I'm feeling kind of blue
I'm on my long journey home

It's dark and it's raining and I've got to go home
Got to go home, boy, got to go home
It's dark and it's raining and I've got to go home
I'm on my long journey home

Under the Double Eagle

The Unfortunate Brakeman

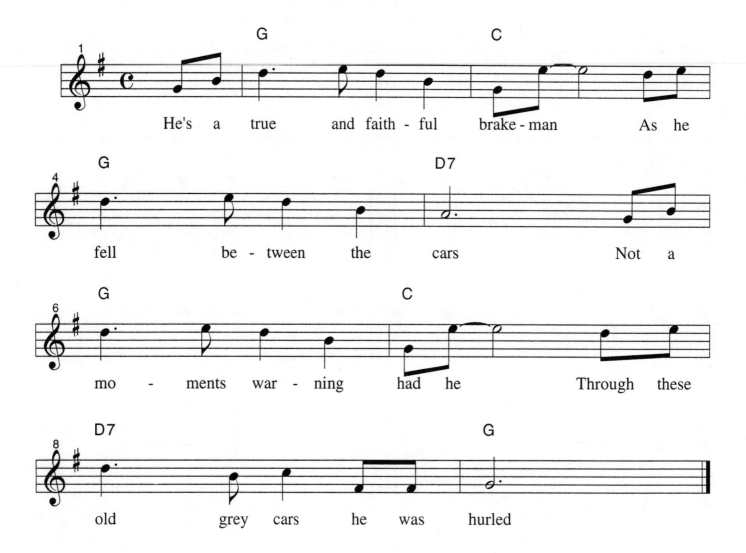

He's a true and faith-ful brake-man As he fell be-tween the cars Not a mo-ments war-ning had he Through these old grey cars he was hurled

He's a brave young engineerman
At the age of twenty-one
As he fell down from his engine
Crying well what have I done

Have I killed my faithful brakeman
Could it be that he will die
Oh I did my best to save him
But I could not stop in time

See the car was pressing o'er him
O'er his mangled body and head
See his sister bending o'er him
Crying brother are you dead

Kind sister yes I'm dying
Going to join some better shores
Tell my buddies on the T.C.
That I'll never see no more

Sister when you see my brother
These few words I'll send to him
Tell him never to venture braking
If he does his life will end

After these few words were spoken
Then he clasped his hands to his breast
And the spirit all had left him
And his soul had gone to rest

Wabash Blues

Wabash Cannonball

From the great At - lan - tic O - cean to the wide Pa - ci - fic shore From the
New York flo - wing moun - tains to the South - lands by the Shore She's
migh - ty tall and hand - some and she's known quite well by all She's the
reg - u - lar com - bi - na - tion she's the Wa - bash Can - non ball

Oh the eastern states are dandies, so the western people say
Chicago, Rock Island, St. Louis by the way
To the lakes of Minnesota, where the rippling waters fall
No changes to be taken on the Wabash Cannonball

Chorus:
Listen to the jingle, the rumble and the roar
As she glides along the woodland, o'er hills and by the shore
She climbs the flowery mountains, hear that lonesome hobo squall
She glides along the woodland, the Wabash Cannonball

Here's to Daddy Clayton, may his name forever be
And long be remembered in the courts of Tennessee
For he is the good old rounder, `til the curtain `round him falls
He'll be carried back to victory on the Wabash Cannonball

I have rode the I.C. Limited, also the Royal Blue
They cross the eastern states on that old car number two
I have rode those highball trains from coast to coast that's all
But I have found no equal to the Wabash Cannonball
Chorus

Walking Boss

When I asked that boss-
Man for a job
I said I want a job
He said son, what can you do

I can line up track
I can line up track
I can pull a jack
I can pick and shovel too
Chorus

I worked one day
Just one hard day
And draw no pay
Then go lay in the shanty two
Chorus

Waltz in D

We Met in the Saddle

This mor-ning is Mon - day De - cem-ber Nine - teen

The judge and the ju - ry are wai-ting for me

I'm go-ing to face them my sto-ry to tell

At eight when they o - pen the door of my cell

There was a fair maiden I learned to love well
On a ranch out in Texas, just north of Crowell
We met in the saddle at the O.B. round-up
A beautiful cowgirl, the kind you would trust

She rode a black stallion, as black as the night
As hot as the six-gun she wore on her right
I told her I loved her, as I ever knew
That we could be married in the fall of the year

But I love another, she quickly replied
The son of Monchongo, the chief of the tribe
She saw I was angry and started to run
And begging for mercy at the point of my gun

As I pulled the trigger, the dear thing turned cold
Her soul left the canyon as I watched her fall
As I watched her struggle and die at my feet
The name of her lover she tried to repeat

When I heard the verdict, I will not deny
The crime I committed but I will reply
For the sake of Monchongo and my angel bride
I'll labor in prison the rest of my life

123

What's the Matter With the Mill

That's my gal, she's the one who did it
She began to like it and just couldn't quit it
Chorus

She's got skin that you love to touch
But I bet that you don't touch much
Chorus

Old Uncle Buck, `bout ninety-six
Just got back from getting it fixed
Chorus

Two old maids in a folding bed
One rolled over and the other one said...
Chorus

(Play the Chicken Reel in A)

Makes no difference how you feel
You won't play that Chicken Reel
Chorus

Whiskey Before Breakfast

When I'm Gone, Don't You Grieve

Well I went down-town fee-lin' migh-ty fun-ny
Found a lit-tle pock-et book and it was full of mo-ney Po-
lice come a-long said lay it down son-ny And I
told you not to grieve af-ter me
When I'm gone don't-cha don't-cha grieve
When I'm gone don't-cha don't-cha grieve

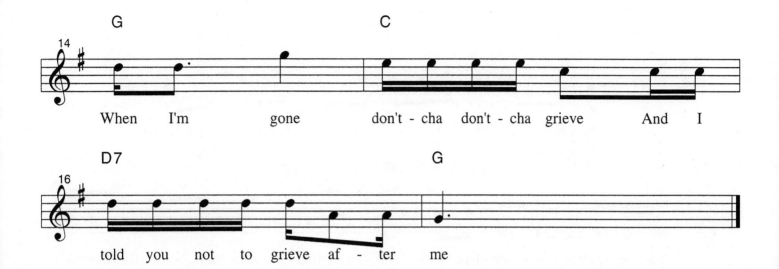

When I'm gone don't-cha don't-cha grieve And I told you not to grieve af-ter me

Went downtown, stayed all night
Said it was a quarter and I told him alright
Jumped into bed and I covered my head
And I told him not to grieve after me
Chorus

Got up next morning, thought I would eat
Cakes and pies looked mighty sweet
Jumped on the table and how did I eat
And I told her not to grieve after me
Chorus

Well I got on the train without a cent of money
Conductor came along, he looked mighty funny
Tapped me on the head, said where you going sonny
And I told him not to grieve after me
Chorus

The very next station the conductor put me off
Told him oughtn't done it for I had a bad cough
I looked around and the train pulled off
And I told him not to grieve after me
Chorus

Chorus

White House Blues

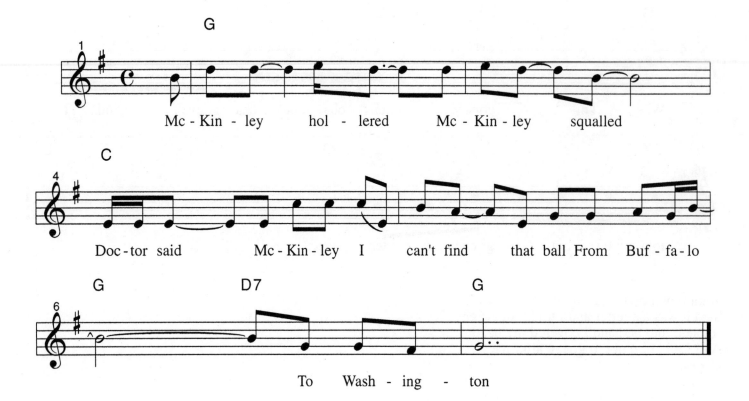

G

Mc - Kin - ley   hol - lered   Mc - Kin - ley   squalled

C

Doc - tor said   Mc - Kin - ley   I   can't find   that ball From   Buf - fa - lo

G   D7   G

To   Wash - ing - ton

Lookit here you rascal, you see what you done
You shot my poor husband with your Iver-Johnson gun
Carry you back to Washington

Along came a lawman, he threw down his badge
He said Mr. McKinley you better cash in your check
You're bound to die, you're bound to die

Yonder comes the train, she's comin' down the line
Blowin' every station, Mr. McKinley's a-dyin'
It's hard times, hard times

Doctor on the horse, he pulled on his mane
Said to that horse you've got to outrun this train
From Buffalo to Washington

Roosevelt in the White House, he's doin' his best
McKinley in the graveyard, he's takin' his rest
He's gone, long old time

Roosevelt's in the White House, drinkin' out of a silver cup
McKinley's in the graveyard, he'll never wake up
He's gone, long old time

Hush up little children, now don't you fret
You'll draw a pension at your papa's death
He's gone, long old time

Wild Horse

Wildwood Flower

Oh I'll twine with my man - gled and wa - ving black hair With the ro - ses so red and the lil - lies so fair And the myr - tle so bright with the em - e - rald dew The pale and the lea - der and eyes look like blue

I will dance and I'll sing and my loss shall be gain
I will charm every heart, in his crown I will sway
When I woke from my dreaming my idol was clay
My portion of loving had all flown away

Oh he taught me to love him and promised to love
And to cherish me over all others above
Though my heart now is wandering no misery can tell
He left me no warning, no words of farewell

Oh he taught me to love him and called me his flower
That's blooming to cheer him through life's dreary hour
I'll live yet to see him regret this dark hour
He won and neglected his pale wildwood flower

The Carter Family's recording sounds in "A." To achieve this, capo on the second fret.

Wish I'd Stayed in the Wagon Yard

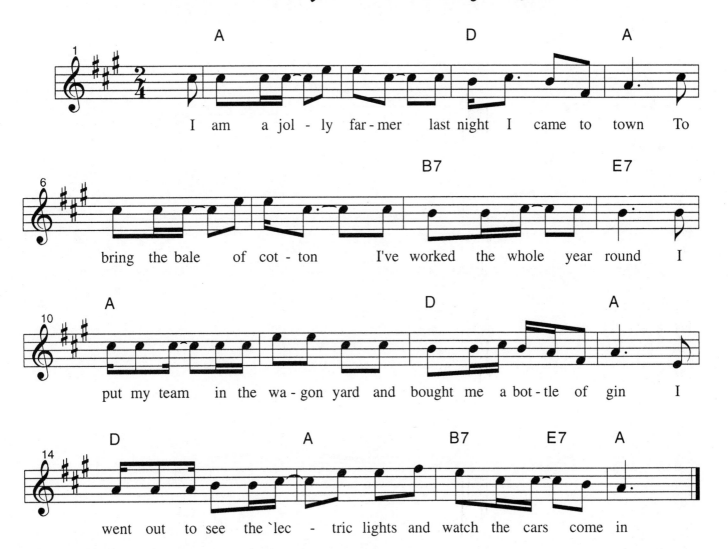

I met a dude out on the street, the clock was striking nine
He says come on old hayseed, take a drink of mine
I must've bought a dozen drinks `cause it hit my pocketbook hard
I wish I'd bought me half a pint and stayed in the wagon yard

Listen to me farmers, I'm here to talk with sense
If you want to see them `lectric lights just look right over the fence
Don't monkey with them city ducks, you'll find they're slick as lard
Just go get you a half a pint and stay in the wagon yard

See I'm a deacon in a hardshell church down near Possum Trot
If the sisters hear about my spree it's bound to make them hot
I went out on a party, I led the pace that killed
When I woke up that gang had gone and left me all the bills

I found them over on the corner, near Soul Salvation Hall
That drunken bunch was out there singing "Jesus Paid it All"
They put me out in a dry bit box, Lord my kibble was hard
I wish I'd bought me a half a pint and stayed in the wagon yard

With My Mother Dead And Gone

I was small but I remember
It was the day my mother died
As I sat there softly weeping
Then she called me to her side

Whispered softly I am going
Where the angels bid me to come
And I hope we'll meet up yonder
When life's work on earth is done
Chorus

Wreck of the Old Ninety-Seven

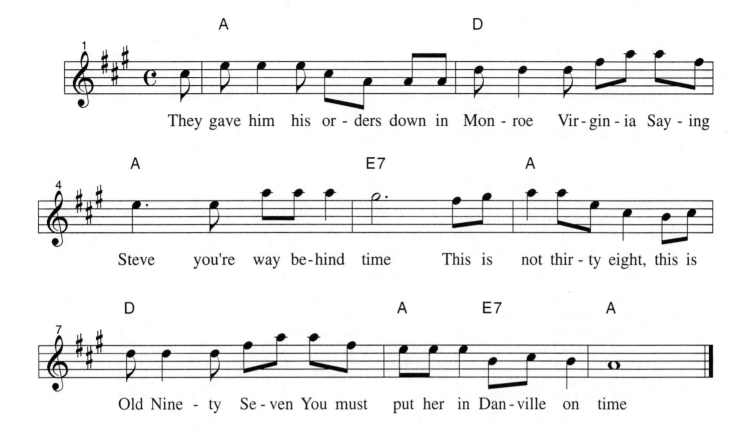

They gave him his or - ders down in Mon - roe Vir - gin - ia Say - ing

Steve you're way be-hind time This is not thir - ty eight, this is

Old Nine - ty Se - ven You must put her in Dan - ville on time

He turned and he said to his big greasy fireman
Just shovel in a little more coal
And when we cross that White Oak Mountain
You can watch Old Ninety-Seven Roll

It's a mighty tough road from Lynchburg to Danville
On a line with a three-mile grade
It was on this grade that he lost his average
You can see what a jump he made

He was going down the grade making ninety miles an hour
When his whistle broke into a scream
They found him in the wreck with his hand on the throttle
He was scalded to death by the steam

Now hear me ladies, for you must take warning
From this time now on
Never speak harsh words to your true loving husband
He may leave you and never return

Key Index

All tunes are in a major key unless otherwise indicated.

A: Beautiful Dreamer; Been to the East, Been to the West; Bill Cheatham; Cindy; Cotton-Eyed Joe (Old-Time Version); Cripple Creek; Cry Holy Unto the Lord; Fire on the Mountain; Nine-Pound Hammer; Old Joe Clark (A Mixolydian); Salt River (A Mixolydian); What's the Matter with the Mill; Wish I'd Stayed in the Wagon Yard; Wreck of the Old Ninety-Seven

B Flat: Tear It Down (Bed Slats and All)

C: All Night Long Blues; Fifteen Cents; Ginseng Blues; Hesitation Blues; My Wife Died Saturday Night; Nobody's Dirty Business; Pass Around the Bottle; Under the Double Eagle

D: Arkansas Traveler; Bile Them Cabbage Down; Bring it on Down to My House; Crawdad; Croquet Habit; Drunkard's Blues (D Minor); Eighth of January; Fiddler's Reel; Fisher's Hornpipe; Ham Beats All Meat; Haste to the Wedding Quadrille; How Long; Ida Red; I'm Troubled; Johnny Lover; L and N Rag; Liberty; Lonesome Road Blues; Make Me a Pallet on the Floor; Maple on the Hill; Midnight on the Stormy Deep; No Disappointment in Heaven; Red River Valley; Saint Anne's Reel; Saro; Shady Grove (Modal Version—D Modal); Soldier's Joy; Somewhere in Tennessee; Stack-O-Lee Blues; Take a Drink on Me; Texas Quickstep; Waltz in "D"; We Me in the Saddle; Whiskey Before Breakfast; With My Mother Dead and Gone

E: Oozlin' Daddy Blues; Rank Strangers to Me; Short Life of Trouble; Wabash Blues

F: Beaumont Rag; Foggy Mountain Top; Oh, Mary Don't Weep; The Titanic; Tom Cat Blues; Wild Horse

G: Alabama Bound; Banks of the Ohio; Blue Eyes; Carroll County Blues (G Mixolydian); Chicken Roost Blues; Columbus Stockade Blues; Cotton-Eyed Joe (Western Swing Version); The Cuckoo (G Modal); Devilish Mary; Don't Grieve After Me; Don't Let the Deal Go Down (Texas Fiddle Tune); Don't Let Your Deal Go Down (Old-Time Song); Dreamy Eyes Waltz; The Girl I Left Behind; Glory to the Lamb; Great Big Taters; Groundhog; He Rambled; Hills of Roane County; Home on the Range; I Want to Go Where Jesus Is; I Wonder if You Feel the Way I Do; I'm a Man of Constant Sorrow (G Modal); Jessie James; June Apple (G Mixolydian); Just a Spoonful; Katy Cline; Keep Knocking; Living Where the Healing Waters Flow; Mama Don't Allow; My Home's Across the Blue Ridge Mountains; Pick Poor Robin Clean; Ragged But Right; Roll 'Em on the Ground; Roll in My Sweet Baby's Arms; Shady Grove; Sleep, Baby Sleep; Sourwood Mountain; Sweet Sunny South; Texas Hambone Blues; There's a Brownskin Gal Down the Road Somewhere; Turkey in the Straw; Two Dollar Bill; The Unfortunate Brakeman; Wabash Cannonball; Walking Boss (G Modal); When I'm Gone, Don't You Grieve; White House Blues; Wildwood Flower

Finding Recordings

The following are some record labels which produce reissues of classic country, blues, bluegrass and western swing:

Arhoolie:

    An eclectic label which has put out some very interesting releases. Unlike some other labels, when Arhoolie reissues material from its LP catalog they consistently add a substantial amount of material—virtually all of their CDs are over seventy minutes in length, and the liner notes are usually quite good. Carter Family fans will enjoy *The Carter Family on Border Radio—1939* (Arhoolie CD 411) which includes "I'm Thinking Tonight of My Blue Eyes" and "Maple on the Hill." They have recently released a CD of Cliff Carlisle recordings (Arhoolie CD 7039) which includes a version of "Columbus Stockade Blues." Their web site (http://www.arhoolie.com/) has a complete catalog.

Bear Family:

    A German label known for thorough box sets of classic performers with excellent liner notes and illustrations. Their Jimmy Rodgers set is the most comprehensive available (containing tracks not included in the Rodgers CDs released by Rounder), as is their box set of the Louvin Brothers. They've just released a box set of Cliff Bruner recordings. See their web site (http://www.bear-family.de/) for a full catalog.

Columbia/ Legacy (Sony):

    Their "Roots and Blues" series is a very good reissue series, the best of any major label. Their CDs are reasonably priced, widely available, and consistently interesting. Particularly strong is the two-CD *White Country Blues (1926-1928): A Lighter Shade of Blue* collection (Columbia/ Legacy CD C2K 47466) assembled by old-time music authority Charles Wolfe. The collection includes Cliff Carlisle's "Chicken Roost Blues" and "Tom Cat Blues" as well as Narmour and Smith's "Carroll County Blues" and Bill Cox and Cliff Hobbs' "Oozlin' Daddy Blues." Also noteworthy is their reissue of Mississippi John Hurt's 1928 recordings (CK 64986) which includes "Stack O' Lee," "Nobody's Dirty Business" and a version of "Make Me a Pallet on the Floor" (under the title "Ain't No Tellin'"). Legacy has also released some good early jazz titles. Their web site (http://www.music.sony.com/Music/ArtistInfo/Legacy/RootsNBlues/) has a complete listing of available titles.

Country Routes/Krazy Kat/Flyright:

All are part of Interstate Music (UK). They have released a number of CDs of old-time country music and western swing which draw heavily from radio transcriptions and small label releases. Many performers who have been ignored by other labels are covered on Country Routes and Krazy Kat CDs. Particularly good are CDs of Johnnie Lee Wills (KKCD 18) and *Jitterbug Jive: Hot Texas Swing 1940-1941* (KKCD 19), as well as *Western Swing on the Radio* (RFD CD 07) and *Cliffie Stone Radio Transcriptions 1945-1949* (RFD CD 08). For a catalog, write to Interstate Music Ltd., 20 Endwell Road, Bexhill-On-Sea, East Sussex TN40 1EA, England.

County:

County was once the most prolific reissuer of old-time music, although their output has declined over the years. The County Historical Series of LPs contained some very interesting releases, most of which unfortunately haven't found their way to CD and are very difficult to find. They've released two volumes of Charlie Poole on CD (County CD 3501 and 3508), which include songs such as "Sweet Sunny South," "Don't Let Your Deal Go Down," "White House Blues," "Wild Horse," "He Rambled," and a version of "Hesitation Blues" (under the title "If the River Was Whiskey"). They've also put out one CD (County CD 3509) of the Skillet Lickers (the only CD of their works which I am aware of), which includes "Devilish Mary" and "Soldier's Joy," as well as two very good CDs of the Delmore Brothers (County CD 110 and 116). They run a mailorder service for old-time music and bluegrass (see below) and have a catalog on the World Wide Web (http://www.countysales.com/).

Rounder:

In the 1970s, Rounder was among the best labels for reissues of old-timey and bluegrass music. The quality of their reissues has declined dramatically in the CD era, and the majority of their most interesting LPs have not yet been reissued on CD. At a time when other labels are putting over twenty tracks on each CD, Rounder seldom includes more than sixteen. They have recently reissued the "Complete" Victor recordings of Jimmy Rodgers and the Carter Family using this tactic to spread the material over more CDs. On a more positive note, Rounder has released several CDs by the Whitstein Brothers, a contemporary duet in the classic tradition of the Blue Sky Boys and the Louvin Brothers. Especially good is their *Old Time Duets* CD (Rounder CD 0264), which includes performances of "We Met in the Saddle," "Somewhere in Tennessee," "Maple on the Hill," and "I'm Troubled." A Rounder catalog is available on the World Wide Wed at (http://harp.rounder.com/contents.htm).

Smithsonian Folkways:

Folkways has released some very good CDs recently, including some expanded versions of items from their LP catalog. Bluegrass fans will like the two Bill Monroe CDs, *Off the Record.* The first CD features live recordings with the Bluegrass Boys, and contains performances of "Fire on the Mountain," "Cotton-Eyed Joe," "White House Blues" and "Roll in My Sweet Baby's Arms." The second CD contains duets with Doc Watson, and includes performances of "Foggy Mountain Top," "Soldier's Joy," "Midnight on the Stormy Deep," Banks of the Ohio," "Fire on the Mountain," and "Turkey in the Straw." Fans of the great guitar picker Doc Watson will also enjoy *The Doc Watson Family* (SF 40012), which contains performances of "Groundhog," "I'm Troubled," "Shady Grove" and "The Cuckoo Bird," as well as the two-CD set *The Original Folkways Recordings of Doc Watson and Clarence Ashley* (SF CD 40029) which includes "Walking Boss," "Short Life of Trouble," and "My Home's Across the Blue Ridge Mountains." Folkways has recently released two CDs of the excellent revival group the New Lost City Ramblers, *Out Standing in Their Field* (SF CD 40040) and *The Early Years: 1958-1962* (SF CD 40036). Also interesting and worthwhile are the greatly expanded CD version of John Cohen's classic *Mountain Music of Kentucky* (containing an hour of material not included on the original LP) and a CD of Bascom Lamar Lunsford, *Ballads, Banjo Tunes, and Sacred Songs of Western North Carolina.* See their web site (http://www.si.edu/folkways/) for more information.

Yazoo:

Has one of the largest catalogs of early blues reissues, as well as a few old-time titles. Many of the tunes in this book can be found on the two-volume *Music of Kentucky* series, including Emry Arthur's "I'm a Man of Constant Sorrow" and "Short Life of Trouble," as well as the Kentucky Ramblers' "The Unfortunate Brakeman," "With My Mother Dead and Gone," "Ginseng Blues" and "Glory to the Lamb." The set also includes Ernest Phipps and his Holiness Quartet performing "I Want to Go Where Jesus Is" and "Don't Grieve After Me," and Alex Hood's Railroad Boys performing "L and N Rag." Also of interest is the three-volume set *Before the Blues*, which contains Charlie Jordan's performance of "Just a Spoonful," Eck Robertson playing "There's a Brownskin Girl Down the Road Somewhere," Luke Jordan's performance of "Pick Poor Robin Clean," Taylor's Kentucky Boys playing "Sourwood Mountain," and Frank Stokes' version of "How Long." Fans of jug band music will enjoy Yazoo's CDs of the Memphis Jug Band, Canon's Jug Stompers and Clifford Hayes and the Dixieland Jug Blowers. Yazoo operates a mailorder service (see below). A complete catalog can be found at their web site (http://www.yazoobluesmailorder.com).

A few more things worth mentioning:

Capitol has released some good things from its vaults, most notably a series of inexpensive Louvin Brothers reissues with excellent liner notes by Charles Wolfe and a great CD of Tex Williams recordings (Capitol CD 36184). Document, which has primarily released early blues music, has just put out a CD of old-time music from West Virginia (DO CD 8004) which includes Frank Hutchison. RCA has recently started reissuing some of the classic blues released on its Bluebird label (with CDs of Sonny Boy Williamson and Tampa Red, among others), and hopefully they will explore their vaults for early country stuff soon (their LP collections of performers such as the Monroe Brothers and Bill Boyd and his Cowboy Ramblers have long been out of print).

Those interested in learning more about western swing are encouraged to start with the recordings of Bob Wills and his Texas Playboys or Milton Brown and his Musical Brownies. The complete recordings of Milton Brown have been issued as a five-CD set by Texas Rose (Texas Rose CD 1-5), which includes versions of "Bring it on Down to My House," "Hesitation Blues," "Texas Hambone Blues," "Under the Double Eagle," "Wabash Blues," and "When I'm Gone Don't You Grieve." Bob Wills reissues are fairly abundant, although the uninitiated should be wary of his later (late 1940's on) material, as it tends to be rather uneven in quality. Edsel has released *Your Friendly King of Western Swing* (Nest CD 905), a CD containing highlights from Wills 1940's radio transcriptions (including western swing versions of "Cotton Eyed Joe" and "Cindy") which is a good place for newcomers to start. Rhino has released *Bob Wills & His Texas Playboys: Anthology (1935-1973)* (Rhino CD 70744) as well as many volumes of *The Tiffany Transcriptions*, and Columbia has several inexpensive CDs of classic Wills recordings available.

Among modern revivalists of early country styles, Doc Watson is king. He has recorded for a number of different labels (including Folkways, Vanguard, United Artist and Sugar Hill), often accompanied by his late son Merle. Watson's repertoire is broad, covering old-time tunes, sacred music, blues, western swing, commercial country and bluegrass, and he has recorded many of the tunes in this book. The four-CD set *The Vanguard Years* (Vanguard CD 155/158) is an excellent introduction to his work.

If you can't find good music at a local record store, the following are good mailorder services. Roots and Rhythm publishes a catalog/ newsletter with well-written reviews of the stuff they carry.

County Sales
P.O. Box 191
Floyd, Virginia 24091
Phone: (540) 745-2001
World Wide Web: http://www.countysales.com

Roots and Rhythm
P.O. Box 2216
San Leandro, CA 94577
Phone: (510) 614-5353
World Wide Web: http://www.bluesworld.com/roots.html

Yazoo Mailorder
PO Box 1004, Cooper Station
New York, NY 10276-1004
Phone: (212) 253-6624
World Wide Web: http://www.yazoobluesmailorder.com

The author wishes to thank William Bay, Kristin Hofer, Judith McCulloh, Larry Gushee, Bill Whitmer, Joe Charboneau, his family, and all the string band folks.